T0326651

Int Interventions | AR Adaptive Reuse

Editors In Chief:
Markus Berger
Liliane Wong

Graphic Design Editor:
Ernesto Aparicio

Int|AR is an annual publication by the editors in chief: Markus Berger + Liliane Wong, and the Department of Interior Architecture, Rhode Island School of Design.

Members of the Advisory Board:

-Heinrich Hermann, Adjunct Faculty, RISD; Head of the Advisory Board, Co-Founder of Int|AR

-Uta Hassler, Chair of Historic Building Research and Conservation, ETH Zurich.

-Brian Kernaghan, Professor Emeritus of Interior Architecture, RISD

-Niklaus Kohler, Professor Emeritus, Karlsruhe Institute of Technology.

-Dietrich Neumann, Royce Family Professor for the History of Modern Architecture and Urban Studies at Brown University.

-Theodore H M Prudon, Professor of Historic Preservation, Columbia University; President of Docomomo USA.

-August Sarnitz, Professor, Akademie der Bildenden Künste, Wien.

-Friedrich St. Florian, Professor Emeritus of Architecture, RISD.

-Wilfried Wang, O'Neil Ford Centennial Professor in Architecture, University of Texas, Austin; Hoidn Wang Partner, Berlin.

Layout + Design_Mukul Chakravarthi, Xiangyu Liu

Editorial + Communications Assistant_Libby Smith

Cover Design_Ernesto Aparicio, Mukul Chakravarthi

Cover Photo_*Aura*, An installation by Edoardo Tresoldi at the Le Bon Marché Rive Gauche, Paris, France

Photograph by © Roberto Conte

Inner Cover Photos_Markus Berger, Liliane Wong

Copyediting_Amy Doyle

Printed by SYL, Barcelona

Distributed by Birkhäuser Verlag GmbH, Basel P.O. Box 44, 4009 Basel, Switzerland,

Part of Walter de Gruyter GmbH, Berlin/Boston

Int|AR Journal welcomes responses to articles in this issue and submissions of essays or projects for publication in future issues. All submitted materials are subject to editorial review. Please address feedback, inquiries, and other material to the Editors, Int|AR Journal, Department of Interior Architecture, Rhode Island School of Design, Two College Street, Providence, RI 02903 www.intar-journal.edu, email: INTARjournal@risd.edu

CONTENTS

04 EDITORIAL

INFORMAL ANNEXATIONS 06 Rafael Luna

HOLDING GROUND 14 Pari Riahi

PHANTOM MARKETS AND GHOST BOOTLEGGERS 22 STORYTELLING AS DESIGN
Liz Teston

RESTORATION IN HISTORICAL PERSPECTIVE 28 BETWEEN MEANING AND PRACTICE
Philip Jacks

INVESTIGATIONS: BETWIXT AND BETWEEN 36 Anne West

ABSENT MATTER 44 AN INTERVIEW WITH EDOARDO TRESOLDI
Liliane Wong

THE SONIFEROUS LANDSCAPE 58 A NEW UNDERSTANDING OF THE SUBLIME
Rana Kamal Abudayyeh and Kramer Woodard

BETWEEN THE SACRED AND THE MUNDANE 68 Alok Bhasin and Puja Anand

CULTURAL AMBASSADORS 74 ALLOPATRIC ADAPTIVE REUSE AND SECONDARY NARRATIVES
Hongjiang Wang

INTERSTITIAL PRACTICES 84 THE STRATEGY OF THE IN-BETWEEN
Madalina Ghibusi, Jacopo Leveratto

IN SEARCH OF SPATIAL NARRATIVES 90 Andreas Müller

LOOKING FROM THE VOIDS IN-BETWEEN 98 Géraldine Borio

SCRATCH, DRAW AND WRITE 108 NARRATIVES ON URBAN CANVASES
Markus Berger

SEARCHING FOR THE IN-BETWEEN

by MARKUS BERGER

Exploring our built environment for traces of human presence and interaction, as well as elements of intervention and change, we discover physical transformations in layers of added and subtracted material deposits. While such transformations are often times caused by natural occurrences, we find human interventions, both deliberate and unplanned. Amidst all of these material transformations, life unfolds in regular and irregular patterns, revealing stories that have been drawn from our neighborhoods, buildings, rooms, nooks or anything in between.

In the inaugural issue of Int|AR, published in July 2009, we defined adaptive reuse and interventions to include: "… not only the reuse of existing structures, but also the reuse of materials, transformative interventions, continuation of cultural phenomena through built infrastructure, connections across the fabric of time and space, and preservation of memory – all of which result in densely woven narratives of the built environment with adaptive reuse as their tool." In the ten years since, we have aimed to investigate very specific topics and address questions relating to this emerging field of architectural reuse and design. As researchers who teach between the practice of architecture and interior design, we felt it necessary to further explore aspects of the many conditions that are neither in one nor the other. In a sense, the name of this journal with its reference to intervention - *intervene* in Latin signifying "to come between"- already speaks to an examination of the "in-between" condition. This volume offers contributions from authors who debate this topic and present multi-faceted insights for discourse of the subject in future design investigations.

One of the primary investigations in the articles relates to defining the IN-BETWEEN in the urban context. Through the work of three different authors, we offer global viewpoints on this subject, from Europe to Asia.

The article, "Interstitial Practices," examines the re-activation of urban interstices through strategies of the In-Between in the context of European cities such as Ponta Delgada, Portugal. "Looking from the Voids In-between" is an exploration of the elderly population in a community that finds liberation by inserting their own urban infill into the derelict systems of Hong Kong's residential streets. "Informal Annexations" investigates existing city grid types and posits the need for new urban typologies found in interventions in between the grids of Seoul, Korea.

Similarly, authors explored the tangible and the intangible conditions of our built environment. "Between the Sacred and the Mundane" studies the secular and religious in the case of the Ghats of Varanasi within permanent and temporary settings. In "Phantom Markets and Ghost Bootleggers" collage and narrative are co-joined to explore the connection between memory and perception and its potential for informing installations and interventions. "Betwixt and Between" investigates the ambiguities of the liminal space between intellectual and emotional responses. Our interview with the artist Eduardo Tresoldi examines questions that are situated between matter and space, the classical and contemporary, and the present and the absent.

Several essays probe the relationship between architecture, nature and society: "Cultural Ambassadors" addresses the concept of secondary narratives of ancient dwellings in Huizhou, China through relocation and reconstruction; "The Soniferous Landscape" instead investigates the disconnect between humans and nature by and through technology; "Holding Ground" examines the constellation of social housing projects and public grounds in the suburbs of Paris, with the intention of locating and identifying transitional spaces. Themes between the image, the word and the world at large are also reviewed: "Restoration in Historical

Practice: Between Meaning and Practice" looks at the origins of definitions and delves into in-between terminology to define the practices of conservation, preservation and adaptive reuse. "In Search of Spatial Narratives" investigates the nature of narrative and the role of the image in architecturally designed spaces. Common to all the articles is the investigation of the in-between condition; as one related to spaces; as ideas filled with ambiguity and uncertainty; as thought and emotion provoking reflections between built and unbuilt territory; as that hovering between creation and destruction. The in-between explores the intersections of paradigms versus styles, and utility versus beauty. The in-between brings out oppositional and complementary aspects between the physical and the virtual, the old versus the new.

The photo essay, "Scratch, Draw and Write: Narratives on Urban Canvases," is one such investigation through the medium of graffiti and street art. Conducted at different scales within the urban context, material as surface, object and building mediates the many aspects of the in-between through individual and societal storytelling in the public realm. Legal, participatory and formal issues come together to form our experiences within our daily built environment,

a setting where the narratives of individuals and society as a whole can be expressed.

In investigating the conditions, forces and narratives that define the "in-between," we explore the medium in which they occur. These can be the skins, perimeters, boundaries, edges or membranes that surround us, or the city grids, zoning laws, objects, buildings and materials in which we interact. Making interventions here draws us into the ambiguities, uncertainties, accumulations and amalgamations of the worlds in-between.

ENDNOTES:

1. Markus Berger, Heinrich Hermann, and Liliane Wong, "Editorial," Int|AR, Journal of Interventions and Adaptive Reuse, Volume 01 (Autumn 2009): 4.

2 OED, To come in or between so as to affect, modify, or prevent a result, action, etc.; Oxford English Dictionary, accessed March 2019, https://0-www-oed-com.librarycat.risd.edu.

Abandoned watertower at Telliskivi in the city of Tallinn, Estonia

INFORMAL ANNEXATIONS

by RAFAEL LUNA

A critical development occurred during the 19th century in the spatial relationships of our cities when the paradigm shifted from city form to city management. The parcelization of the city by the implementation of grid standards allowed multiple cities to produce a management tool for taxation and property control. It was popularized by the iconic projects of the Commissioners' Plan of 1811, Haussmann's plan for Paris in the 1850s, and, most importantly, theorized and published as the "General Theory of Urbanization" by Ildefons Cerda for the expansion of Barcelona. These models were repeated all over the globe as urbanization expanded. Yet parcelization could not have foreseen the informalities of the city in the space that happens between parcels and between buildings. Such is the case in Seoul, in the district of Hongdae where the leftover space between the parcel and the building is appropriated as an interior extension, giving rise to a whole neighborhood economy of illegal marketable space. These spaces are used as shops, restaurants, galleries, through an extension of the ground level. This essay will review how the in-between space has not only produced an interesting neighborhood condition but a variety of interior spaces that have adapted to maximize the residual spaces of parcels.

In the continuing process of urbanization, much emphasis has been placed on the development of city form through the implementation of grid design. The grid has been equated to a method for establishing city form, as well as a political tool for managing the growth of cities. The grid in itself could be studied independently as an urban artifact with its roots as a control tool developed by the Roman Empire during its expansive colonization.

The parameters that founded each of these imperial colonies followed two axes; the *cardo* and *decumanus* embedded a directional logic onto the system with parallel streets, a system of subdivisions for development and public squares. Aside from providing a geometrical strategy for organizing citizens, the formation of these cities through the grid developed the important distinction between *res publica* and *res privata*. These Latin terms defined that which is public and that which is private. They politicized the land and the managerial aspect of maintaining such land; that which was maintained by the state would be considered *res publica*, or public with access to all. This is one of the embedded fundamental aspects that needs to be addressed when discussing the nature of our cities - both as a separation of privacies through the grid and the resulting implications on the efficiency of urban space. The grid, therefore, should be defined not as a direct geometric operation of design that is imposed on a field, but as the primary infrastructural network that shapes the public realm of a city and its parcelized privacies. The space in-between the parcels is arguably the most important factor in defining the city, as it represents the area of discrepancy between the public infrastructure and private buildings. In-between the parcels and buildings exists the political, contested space between private land and public access - the space for appropriation. It represents a hidden value of urban efficiency, one that unearths the inadequacies of understanding a city as fixed spaces through grids and parcelization.

Understanding urban efficiency through the in-between space created by the parcelization process requires a review of contemporary methodologies for

Storefront extensions hide the legal border of buildings and give the appearance of a larger store

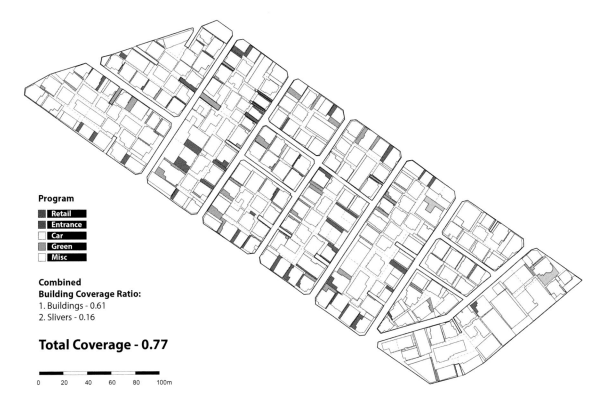

Program

- Retail
- Entrance
- Car
- Green
- Misc

**Combined
Building Coverage Ratio:**
1. Buildings - 0.61
2. Slivers - 0.16

Total Coverage - 0.77

0	20	40	60	80	100m

reading a city. Systems like GIS (geographic information system), for example, have been in development since the 1960s. They record what has been legally documented as public infrastructure, the subdivisions of parcels, and the perimeter of buildings inside parcels. Although GIS is the most popular method for visualizing and working with open source data for mapping, for architects it is mainly used to demonstrate building coverage area and two dimensional urban forms, such as a Nolli map. Urban efficiency in this scenario could be described through the density of the urban fabric of a city as an indicator of walkability and, therefore, density of amenities for occupancy. In his book *Walkable City: How Downtown Can Save America, One Step at a Time*, Jeff Speck argues for the need of a healthy building density that allows for higher usability of the space by its residents.[1] The further the separation of the in-between space of buildings, the less efficient the city, as walking distances between buildings are longer and the city more car-oriented. This argument is exemplified by projects such as the "taxonomy of urban fabrics," generated by the urbanization.org group at the Institute for Advanced Architecture of Catalonia.[2] The intent of this project is to create a classification of urban fabrics from around the world as an open source to allow for collaborative comparative studies. Although a comparative study of this kind would provide valid information regarding densities, it would not demonstrate the in-between condition that occurs by informal occupations.

The ad-hoc appropriations of public space for private use are common in a dense city like Seoul. In their book *Borrowed City*, Bruno, Carena, and Kim analyze the condition of appropriation of the public space in Seoul as a social contract among the residents and local government. "Borrowed City can be simply defined as the way private citizens use public space for their own personal benefit... Most of these "negotiated" activities are illegal, but at the same time they are the result of a mutual agreement among citizens, which is a fundamental process in any democracy. For this reason, in a public space debate, informal occupations should be considered more as a resource to exploit than a problem to eradicate."[3] "Borrowed City" describes the condition in Seoul that exists out of the demarcated limits of a grid. Pop-up shops or tents may happen on the sidewalk, alleys, or between buildings as common occurrences regardless of their legality. Although they are not accounted for as legal building spaces or registered commercial activity, they provide amenities that may not be present inside legal buildings but are ingrained in the daily use of the city.

Another methodology to note is the mapping generated through the visualization of big data. In computation, big data refers to large data sets that could be analyzed to reveal patterns. These data sets have been incrementally increasing through the internet and the process of digitalizing our environments. The Civic Data Design Lab at MIT has been producing such mappings to evaluate the real estate speculative development occurring in China.[4] The visualization of data sets from

Diagram of in-between programming of Hongdae Block

social network apps reveals urban voids. These areas lack amenities and therefore become unsustainable communities, contributing to a phenomenon labeled as Ghost Cities. Urban efficiency is presented as a model of proximity to amenities for local residents.

These methodologies present an understanding of urban efficiency as an expression of density and proximities within legal parameters, be it recorded survey of buildings or licensed business operations. These methodologies operate within the public and private limits demarcated by the grid system. Yet in a dense urban environment, the public boundaries are sometimes blurred through appropriations of the in-between spaces as shown in studies like *Borrowed City*. These appropriations or occupations uncover the need for an additional understanding of the in-between, not just as a function of space but also of time. In 2002, Groupe e2 formed an international ideas competition to explore the notion of the in-between urban condition. Although the connotation of the "in-between" in the brief may have been preconceived to connote the space between two things, Bernard Tschumi offered a separate observation of the importance of understanding the in-between also as a time reference.[5] The in-between can be conceptualized as the progressive layering effect that builds the city over time, implying a new dimension; the lack of this dimension in the Nolli plan methodology explains its failure to capture the city in its totality, one including ad-hoc occupancies and temporal events.

The inadequacies of understanding a city through its grid and parcelization as fixed spaces rather than its in-between spaces are furthered studied by Solomon, Wong, and Frampton in their book *Cities Without Ground: A Guide to Hong Kong's Elevated Walkways*,[6] a demonstration of the endless three-dimensional connections that occur in Hong Kong's pedestrian networks. The in-between space is completely blurred through the appropriation of public infrastructure for private commercial use. The space between buildings becomes irrelevant as a two-dimensional ground condition because public infrastructure is extended into the private interior spaces, offering a continuous urban experience instead of a compartmentalized parcelization of two-dimensional space.

In both scenarios of appropriations, Seoul and Hong Kong, the need for space has led to an understanding of urban efficiencies beyond the political implication of the grid. The grid still represents the bundled, sunken investment of a city with an intrinsic path-dependency and limited possibilities of change to its formal structure. This implies that once a grid is laid out variation can only come from its subdivisions and the evolution of the architecture currently seen occurring in dense Asian cities through informal occupations.

The city of Seoul, for example, experienced a period of rapid urbanization in its postwar of the sixties, seventies, and eighties, which generated a milieu of urban fabrics within the city. The development of the different housing types was a direct response to the rapid incoming and growing population. This led to the production of a quantity of buildings regardless of the quality of urban space. As the city stabilized its growth in becoming a twenty-first century post-industrial cultural city, there has been a growing emphasis on the quality of urban space. In Seoul, this can only be produced through the appropriation of void spaces in the given variety of existing grids.

One specific case study is the dense commercial neighborhood of Hongdae, where the in-between has evolved beyond the parcelization of the grid system to appropriate the setback spaces of buildings as extensions of the interior commercial spaces. Although setback areas are legally owned by the property owner, their purpose is to serve as easements for safe passage in case of emergencies, to separate buildings in case of fire or earthquakes, and to provide natural ventilation and lighting. Setbacks are technically private property but serve a public safety function, making them an ambiguous semi-private space. Bypassing the legality of building within the setbacks, many of the buildings on the main streets of Hongdae extend their volume as commercial sheds using temporal and light materials that afford them a dubious legality.

The presence of these occupations relates to the grid implementation of the neighborhood, which appears on city survey maps during the 1970s. The area is flanked by Hongik University, which was established in 1946, and hints at informal dense settlements that occurred before the development of the parcels. This parcelization process of defining informal settlements within legal parcels resulted in buildings that are separated through setbacks ranging in average from two to four meters. This leaves spaces of one to two meters for each neighbor's side. The area is typologically characterized by lowrise buildings three to four stories high. As the neighborhood continued to densify due to its appeal as an arts and music scene anchored by Hongik University, there was a need for buildings to expand into the only remaining void spaces: the in-between setbacks. Bounded also by the subway Line 2, commuter train Gyeongui–Jungang Line, and the Airport Line to Seoul station, the area thrives with a constant inflow of tourists

and a younger population of students, making the area one of the most active commercial areas in Seoul. In order to benefit the most from this retail context, stores use every available space to capitalize on the display and vending of their merchandise. The mapping of the in-between spaces reveals five typologies of appropriation: retail extension, entrance extension, green space, car oriented spaces, and miscellaneous storage.

The first appropriation type, retail extension, derives from the adaptation of garage spaces and the extension of the ground level storefront. These are the most interesting examples among the five typologies, as the interior volume makes use of the additional setback space for an interior effect. Garages of buildings that are raised on pilotis for ground level parking are transformed into boutique retail spaces. The one meter setback in this example becomes a highlighted rack space, naturally lit through a polycarbonate roof that encloses the setback. This is a typical scenario that technically maintains a

A ground level parking garage transformed into boutique retail space

green space has a larger social role that benefits the neighborhood more than the individual. In the previously mentioned competition from 2002 by Groupe e2, a Japanese entry proposed using these one meter setbacks as a way of creating a perimeter ring of green around Tokyo. As a semi-private space, these slivers, vertical gardens between buildings, could play a larger infrastructural role as green lungs for the city, especially in large cities like Seoul that suffer from pollution and bad air quality.

The fourth adaptation is that of driveways transformed as advertisement entrances instead of for car parking. Due to parcelization, some buildings occupy the middle of the block without any street front other than a narrow driveway. These driveways are highlighted as part of an entrance sequence to commercial spaces in the back. They extend the interior experience to the street.

Lastly, the miscellaneous spaces are used for extra storage or just left empty. The use of light materials like polycarbonate roofing allows inventory to be kept outside of the building. Laundromats, for example, will extend their operations into these spaces, using them for drying racks.

Although this phenomenon seems quite unique to Hongdae with its retail density, this condition is repeated in other neighborhoods like Itaewon or Sinsa-dong, which have similar urban fabric makeup of low-rise buildings separated by two to five meters of shared setbacks. Analysis of the actual usage of setback space among the selected case study blocks in Hongdae indicates about a ten percent increase in usability. This is a higher efficiency of use than that recorded by traditional methods, and it relies on the ingenuity of interior design to work within the legal parameters. This case study also suggests a potential need for understanding the spacing that generates an unplanned urbanity.

In order to compare the condition of the unplanned appropriation of the in-between in relation to grid types, fifteen grid types within a 0.25 km² boundary are compared based on building coverage ratios. These fifteen types of grids represent a cross-section of time in the development of Seoul. The grids closer to the inner core have been in transformation since the inception of Seoul in 1392. The original streams in the inner core formed informal urban fabrics that remain today. The grids further from the inner core represent areas that experienced rapid development during the decades of the sixties, seventies, and eighties. These grids were laid out on empty land as a tabula rasa condition in a "western development" style of regular grids. The variation in distance between buildings among the various grids showcases an interpretation of urban efficiency through appropriation. Areas that already have fifty percent area coverage leave little room for intervention. Yet areas that have very low coverage ratios below twenty percent as in Apgujeong, Yeouido, or Jamsil have separations

legal use. Some of the storefront extensions hide the legal border of the building by constructing a decorated façade, using the additional area to give the appearance of a larger store. Inside, these tend to be covered with polycarbonate roofing to maintain the feel of a naturally lit sliver. Some shed-like setbacks that have more than 2 meters build an enclosure with aluminum panels or light construction as if it were a temporary construction without insulation.

The second appropriation type is the use of the setback as an entrance to the building. Exterior stairs do not count in the calculation of legal FAR (floor area ratio), and by moving the entrance to the second or third floor on the side setback, the ground floor can gain extra square meters of interior retail space.

The third appropriation type includes a social agenda, as the setbacks are used as green space. Because the width of the setbacks would not allow for a proper private garden, the notion of using these spaces as a

between buildings that exceed forty meters. These are areas made up of high-rise apartment complexes inside megablock infrastructure with no clear demarcation of parcelization. These developments resemble socialist blocks such as the Superquadra in Brasilia, where the privatized in-between is completely lost. In his essay on Brasilia in the Typological Urbanism issue of AD,[7] Tarttara explains Lucio Costa's intention of generating a socialist space through the displacement of linear housing blocks, raised on pilotis, in order to democratize the ground as public space. The amenities found on these superquadras follow social infrastructural agendas like public schools, daycare centers, community centers, or athletic facilities, rather than privately developed commercial retail spaces like cafes or restaurants. The relationship of *res publica* and *res privata* is flipped vertically as the entire ground is intended for public use, and private development is lifted to allow unobstructed views and free pedestrian flow throughout the entire block.

The fifteen different grids allow for a conceptualization of the in-between space as a political space based on the distance of separation between buildings. Conceptually, the further away the buildings are from each other, as in Jamsil, Yeouido or Apgujeong, the more the parcelization process is lost. These developments are scaled to the size of the megablock and built as

individual projects. This type democratizes the land and makes appropriations more difficult, while tighter urban fabrics privatize the ground and the subdivisions take on a more important role allowing for free market appropriations.

As discussed by Pier Vittorio Aureli in his description of the grid in the *[re]Form: New Investigations in Urban Form* symposium at Harvard, it is the subdivisions of the grid[8] that become the most important part of shaping the urban form, an idea consistent with gridded development in history. Aureli offers the possibility of escaping the dependency of subdivisions through "island" urban occupations such as the *acampada* in Madrid. These informal settlements, like the Occupy Wall Street (OSW) movements, created urbanities of the in-between informal settlements in urban voids. In cities like Seoul, where informal occupations are not rare, as previously discussed in *Borrowed City*, the island development effect can take place in the large in-between grounds as a second layer of informal amenities.

As a speculative scenario, new smart infrastructures may allow the customization of the urban space. Large open grounds between buildings could potentially allow for informal occupations controlled through digital technologies. Antoine Picon discusses the discrepancy that is occurring between the notion of "smart city" or "smart

The driveway transformed to commercial entrance

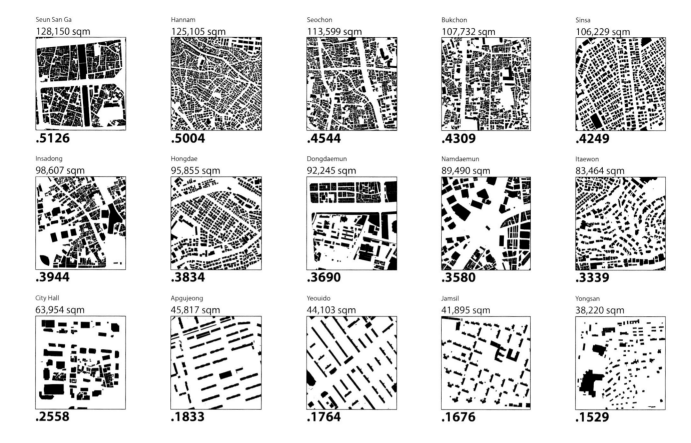

Seun San Ga	Hannam	Seochon	Bukchon	Sinsa
128,150 sqm	125,105 sqm	113,599 sqm	107,732 sqm	106,229 sqm
.5126	**.5004**	**.4544**	**.4309**	**.4249**

Insadong	Hongdae	Dongdaemun	Namdaemun	Itaewon
98,607 sqm	95,855 sqm	92,245 sqm	89,490 sqm	83,464 sqm
.3944	**.3834**	**.3690**	**.3580**	**.3339**

City Hall	Apgujeong	Yeouido	Jamsil	Yongsan
63,954 sqm	45,817 sqm	44,103 sqm	41,895 sqm	38,220 sqm
.2558	**.1833**	**.1764**	**.1676**	**.1529**

infrastructure" and the actual urban makeup.[9] Our cities still maintain a known form based on a grid logic that no longer reflects the advances in technology shaping our daily lives. As previously mentioned, the path dependency of the grid will not allow much of a spatial transformation, but the in-between space of appropriation can quickly become the adaptable space for these new tendencies enabled by the technology of mass customization. The larger in-between spaces could be regulated for other activities, operating as temporal islands as smart devices allow for multiplicity of use for the same setting. Smaller spaces, such as the ones in Hongdae or Sinsa, can also become integrated as virtual commercial spaces. Spaces of one meter to two meters in width can offer the virtual platforms for shopping while the interior displays physical goods. The hidden values of the unaccounted for setback space of the in-between offers a whole new field of operations as an independent layer of the future city.

ENDNOTES:

1 Speck, Jeff. *Walkable City: How Downtown Can save America, One Step at a Time*. New York: North Point Press, 2013. P10

2 http://urbanization.org/project.html?project=5

3 Bruno, Marco, Simone Carena, and Minji Kim. *Borrowed City: Private Use of Public Space in Seoul*. Seoul: Damdi Publishing, 2015. P15

4 http://civicdatadesignlab.mit.edu/#projects/GHOST%20 CITIES%20-%20BEYOND%20THE%20IMAGE

5 Perrault, Dominique, Bernard Tschumi, Michel Desvigne, and Nasrine Seraji-Bozorgzad. *E2: Exploring the Urban Condition*. Paris: Groupe E2, 2002.

6 Frampton, Adam, Jonathan D. Solomon, and Clara Wong. *Cities without Ground: A Hong Kong Guidebook*. Berkley: Oro Editions, 2015.

7 Martino Tarttara, Brasilia's Prototypical Design in *Architectural Design*, January/ February 2011, Volume 209. P.46-55

8 https://youtu.be/0L7Anlsu2A4

9 Picon, Antoine. *Smart Cities: A Spatialised Intelligence*. Chichester: Wiley, 2015. P11-14

14   Cité de L'Abreuvoir, Bobigny, Architect: Emile Aillaud, 1956-1958

HOLDING GROUND

by PARI RIAHI

To lie in shadow on the lawn
By a crumbling wall, pale and withdrawn
...
Rising, to wander in bewilderment
With the sun's dazzle, and the sorry thought
How all our life, and all its labors spent,
Are like a man upon a journey sent
Along a wall that's sheer and steep and
endless, dressed
With bits of broken bottles on its crest.

—Eugenio Montale [1]

Lying in the shadow of a garden wall, partaking the world and observing it, is an experience relatable to many of us, conjoining our memory and imagination to the built environment. The sense of being sheltered is essential in understanding the spatial setting that surrounds us and forms our relationship with others. Abdellatif Kechiche's *Games of Love and Chance* portrays the rehearsal of a play by a group of adolescents at the foot of Les Francs Moisins, a large social housing complex on the outskirts of Paris. [2] As the protagonists thread between the play and real-life, an open amphitheater at the foot at the towers become the space of drama and discovery, a place apart from the confines of each adolescent's home and school. Intrigued by the vast and partly aban-doned outside spaces surrounding the projects, this short photographic-based essay studies the constella-tion of social housing projects and public grounds in the suburbs of Paris in search of transitional spaces that may evoke the experience of being outside while being sheltered by elements of architecture. Focusing on spaces surrounding the housing projects, this essay is keen to identify the different connotations of open and public spaces. It documents different forms of ground, demonstrating the variety, spread and sheer scale of the unoccupied ground that borders the dense housing projects. Observing the scale and ambiguity of the existing ground(s) – whether natural or artificial, transformed or left on its own, soft or hard – and documenting some of its variety may be a critical step in reconfiguring the heritage of the late 20th century.

PROLOGUE

The suburbs of Paris have often been characterized as dysfunctional, violent, and problematic. The "geographic and symbolic" separation of Paris from its suburbs as suggested by Simon Ronai [3] have led to a clear demarcation between the urban and the suburban. This divide also may be extended to one between the modernist heritage of the housing projects and that of the more historic and primarily Haussmannian Paris. Equally, the divide manifests itself between the large-scale housing clusters and the intertwined fabric of the mixed-use city. Those suburban housing projects, built between the First World War and the Seventies, encircle Paris and yet are physically separated from it by the imposing Boulevard Périphérique. As the debates on the social and architectural merits of transforming the suburbs (les banlieues) go on, rethinking these spaces as architectural places is critical. From an architectural point of view, understanding the charged heritage of the recent past as "one of accumulative experimentation and continual revision,"[4] as qualified by Kenny Cupers, becomes more critical, and questions of different degrees of preservation come into play.

Since the inception of the Grand Paris initiative in 2007 and its official inauguration by Nicholas Sarkozy in 2009, the vision for expanding Paris has taken a faster turn. The project to extend the city beyond its historic limit and create a well-connected social, economic and cultural fabric in the Ile de France region has been deployed in different scales and types of action. Theresa Enright observes that while the project is complex and has multiple narrators, Sarkozy had already set many of its objectives, and they have proved difficult to undo.[5] Sarkozy's speech primarily articulated a vision for the city, where the suburbs would be reunited with the center, and the hierarchical relationship between the city and its periphery would be restored. However, easier said than done, the complex fabric of geographical delineation, municipal politics, social and cultural interactions and economic factors pose challenges that defy the unifying gesture to the core. The most recent article by Robert Borloo paints a picture of the inequalities, problems and challenges ahead.[6]

As the Grand Paris [7] initiative unfolds at a rapid pace, and as many as 68 new train and tram stations (as well as new public projects around them) have already been built, preserving or transforming the large housing projects in the suburbs in order to reconnect the fabric of the city to its surroundings has come to include many different possibilities. The extent to which these projects and their surroundings are to be preserved or transformed has been the subject of constant scrutiny. Concrete efforts are currently encompassing any number of the actions, ranging from "residentialisation, rehabilitation, restructuring, construction and reconstruction of the housing projects, creation of roads, defining public spaces, adding urban furniture." [8] While the housing projects are pulled apart, reconfigured and partially or entirely transformed, their surrounding land is often too quickly dismissed or entirely reconfigured through a new landscape intervention.

While projects at the scale of the entire agglomeration aim to connect and cohere to metropolitan Paris, architectural interventions such as Tour Bois-le Prêtre by Frederic Druot, Anne Lacaton and Jean Philippe Vassal in 2013 demonstrate the merit of controlled, minimal and yet profound change. Similar targeted transformations can be imagined for many of these complexes while preserving them to a great extent. This essay looks into the immediate surrounding of the towers as a focus of a careful investigation followed by possible reconfigurations. Investigating the grounds at the foot of these projects will have a lasting impact on transforming the areas for the better. Building on a large series of documentation to capture the current state of a few of these projects, this essay points to the importance of the surroundings, largely gathered under the umbrella of "ground", and their intertwined nature with the architecture they serve.

PROBING THE SUBURBAN VOID

This essay investigates the multi-layered fabric of the built environment as a possible site for interaction and transformation. By examining the immediate environment surrounding the projects, these grounds of different forms and scale are identified as a first place for reconfiguration. In order to do so, they first have to be understood and appreciated for what they are: inherently different from the public and open spaces of the city. Looking into the sheer scale of open spaces in any given suburb demonstrates that the proportions and distribution of figure/ ground, as we understand them within the urban fabric, no longer apply. In looking closer to explore the distribution between the figure and the ground, we observe that the ground – even when designated with certain functions – is often part of a void, countering the masses that pierce the horizon and densely populate the land. The void is an all-encompassing three-dimensional non-functional space, which is often as large as the housing complexes are, and its distribution is as consuming as the built space.

The Disappearing Threshold: La Boulevard Périphérique

The Liminal: La Cité Arago, Saint Ouen, Architect: Paul Chemetov

The Framed: La Maladrerie, Aubervilliers, Architect: Renée Gailhoustet, 1975-1986

Countering the formed, built, and occupiable, the void presents itself as an imposing presence, a force to be reckoned with.

Embracing the contrast between the center and the periphery, Manuel de Sola Morales observes that 'splendid' or 'cursed' peripheral zones are primarily shaped by political forces that govern them.[9] This observation still resonates with the suburbs of Paris against the odds of time and changes that have taken place in the metropolitan area. The economical and social make of the suburbs have contributed to complex environments that appear to float as fragmented clusters around the historical city. Sola Morales argues that within the peripheral zones, the social spaces that exist are fragmented, once again in part because of the political governance of different municipalities. However, he offers that by embracing the distance from the center, as a tool in service of the peripheries, one can counter and test ideas of organizing the city. In particular, he contrasts the quality and scale of the urban void as an exercise that is artificial and subtractive, to that of suburban void, which is a pre-condition created by differences in geographical, judicial and governmental structures. Sola Morales' emphasis is on conflict and opposition as productive forces. He suggests that the distance from the city, as well as the scale of the suburban voids, create opportunities for thinking differently about architectural artifacts, their interrelationship and their role within a larger agglomeration.

The photographs of this essay depict such voids in their multiplicity, demonstrating contained, boundless, indeterminate and transitional conditions. Collectively they demonstrate that distance and scale are the two factors that determine the nature of these voids. If, in urban space, voids alleviate dense urban fabrics, in the suburbs, they morph into larger, amorphous presences

that define the built environment. As the built environment of the suburbs is shaped by repetitious objects and ubiquitous forms, the open and public voids, in their many forms, occupy the landscape without offering a ground for social interactions for the individual, or larger forms of public gathering. While the range covers anything from empty land to over programmed landscapes allocated to different activities, the lack of meaningful space for small or large social interaction is shared between many of these sites.

STAKING THE GROUNDS

Initiating a process of reconfiguration in the areas surrounding the large housing ensembles seems a plausible method to preserve the existing architecture to a large extent. At the same time, it is necessary to address the absence of thresholds and hierarchies that should be in place between the individual spatial needs (such as shelter and privacy) and social needs (freedom, interaction, and being within the public domain). In order to transform the grand gestures of urbanisms in the second half of the 20th century, the first step is to analyze and understand the grounds that surround us within those suburbs. By using photography as a medium, applying a white filter that highlights the ground, and at times subtle changes through collage, the photos depict the over- or under- determinism of these landscapes, their vastness, their composed or abandoned nature, their transitional or stagnant state, and their formless or patterned appearances. They document gradations of lack of intimacy, closeness and connection. Simultaneously the photos depict the dormant beauty of the forms, lines, grids and angles that shape those environments.

The social housing projects, demonstrating different densities and proportions, were examined through the

The Relentless: La Cité des Francs-Moisins, Saint Denis, 1974

lens of photography. The photographs, taken in the span of 2017 and 2018, represent different locations within the North and Northeastern suburbs of Paris: Saint Denis, Saint Ouen, Bobigny, Nanterre and Aubervilliers. They depict the scale, ambiguity and diversity of ground in different locations. The photographs were then re-worked to visually highlight the presence and propor-tion of the occupiable (often hard-scape) ground. Each figure pairs two photographs, attesting to the fact that even within one condition the voids and grounds that surround each project offer more ambiguity and variety. For many of those housing projects, the grounds were initially imagined as "generous, fluid and shared," aspiring to evoke free fields and masses of greenery enveloping the buildings.[10] The social, cultural, and economic unfolding of life in the housing projects failed to coincide with initial architectural aspirations which later proliferated and multiplied–often to the detriment

The Floating: Quartier Pablo Picasso, Nanterre, Architect: Emile Aillaud, 1972-1981

of the initial architectural principles on which they were founded. The ground was often crucial to the evolution of architecture, both in the writings of Le Corbusier and the principals of the Modern Movement.[11]

The Disappearing Threshold
One crosses over a thickened edge to step into the *banlieues*, passing through the conspicuous *Boulevard Périphérique,* the ring road often overtaken by lanes of cars throughout the day. The disappearance of the ground in face of the extreme verticality of the walls, or the horizontality of large housing blocks, is striking. Here the ground is reduced to mere nonexistence, dominated by built infrastructure and architecture. At the foot of the towers or through the maze of entangled cars, the individual fades and the collective disappears. Here, graffiti adorns the walls and disposed goods and trash dance as fading ghosts that occupy the ground.

The Liminal
At the foot of the tall, thin and wide tower designed by Paul Chemetov, the grounds lie in contrast with the dimensions of the building. Primarily understood as a series of framed pathways and controlled spaces for play, the dimensions of the ground are minimized compared with the proportions of the building. While the stratified roof gardens and balconies break down the scale of inhabitation, the absence of different types of open space - off of designated paths - which could serve as potential sites for gathering to and from the building,

is prominent. Here the ground is primarily flat, elements of architecture such as walls, fences, handrails and planters modulate and take the space apart.

The Framed
The stacked layers of the housing project structure the ground. The housing is multi-layered and complex, and the ground moves to the ebb and flow of the small terraces, broken down volumes, and greenery. Surrounded by vegetation at different levels, the public ground is primarily firm, structured and hard, offering a measured datum for the architecture to unravel around it. The ratio of building to ground is modulated and the ground is carved, stacked and defined by the same geometric determination that shapes the architecture. Constantly referring back to the vertical surfaces of the walls, the ground recedes and disappears as layers stacked on top of each other to define the vertical landscape of the project. More coherent in the smaller and confined courtyards, the ground is guided and defined by the ever-changing horizon and the vegetation.

The Relentless
Stretched over the expansive Cité des Francs-Moisins the ground is disengaged and unforgiving. Here the ground is as vast as the complex is large. While there is a seeming abundance of open space, some of which has been overtaken by large surface parking, it is often impossible to be comforted by the presence of the open spaces. Faced with the horizontal spread of the lower

units and the vertical dominance of the higher towers, the ground offers little comfort of shelter. The vast open space at the center of the complex falls short of affording thresholds to break down one's understanding of the space and mediate between the scale of the individual and that of the collective. Instead, it serves as a vast reverse panopticon, within the deserted centralized spaces.

The Floating
Playing on reversals and bordering on pictorial, the overall grounds of the Quartier Pablo Picasso prove ambitious in their desire to be understood as a whole, as a series of images, and in parts, as pockets of landscaped clusters. The playground and large open spaces test the consequences of superimposing visual images on the ground, imaging the project as a work of art, and a series of sculptures, with the buildings playing their part in the overall tableau. While the gentle rolling grounds and the tree clusters create a softer, scaled-down experience for the residents and visitors at the foot of the towers, the large spaces in between the towers float, destabilizing the towers and one's reading of them. Here the extreme verticality of the towers contrasts to the ground on which they are erected.

The Stagnant
Here the ground is abundant and prominent, evoking the cité-jardin, albeit with taller buildings. The expansive grounds, at times occupied by rows and groves of trees and at times covered in grass, are proportionally distributed. However, while the architecture makes attempts to interact with the landscape at many fronts, from the rolling curves of the facades to the sculptural curvature of the tower entrances, to the protrusion of the balconies, to the central open spaces, the grounds feel motionless at times. The grounds' inertness resists offering viable spaces for gathering and play. Here, once again, the open spaces seem to retreat from their ability to mediate between the indoor and the outdoor, the individual and the social.

EPILOGUE
Relating to the elements of a ground, the one we occupy with our body, experience with our senses and interact with through our actions, makes us all the more human. This essay asks whether erasing, underlining, retracing and holding the lines of such grounds within the body of architecture may afford a possibility to redefine the spaces of the *banlieues*. Is it possible to include the vestiges of a recent past – despite their complex history – as part of our architectural heritage in order to safeguard and transform by necessary measures? The photographs depict the ambiguity and sheer presence of the suburban void and show the ground as part of the void that surrounds and sustains the suburban

space. Just as in Kechiche's film, the narrative stretches between the poles of the home (as the space of the individual) and the school (space of the public), while the open amphitheater emerges as the space that liberates and shelters. These grounds might be understood as where the individuals find their voices and face the public sphere on their own term. The photographs presented here are an invitation to look more closely and attentively at an environment that as architects, we might have too quickly dismissed or mislabeled. Nostalgia for the more familiar forms of the historic city aside, these voids, in their complex and fragmented existence, offer possibilities for pause, bewilderment and marvel, by creating grounds from which all forms of interaction, real and imagined, emerge.

ENDNOTES:
1 Eugenio Montale, *Selected Poems* (New York: New Directions Publishing Corporations, 1965), excerpts from "The Wall," 12-15

2 Abdellatif Kechiche, *L'Esquive*, translated in English to the *Games of Love and Chance*, 2002.

3 Simon Ronai, "Paris et la Banlieue: Je t'aime, moi non plus", Herodote, *Revue de Geographie et de Geopolitique*, second trimester, 2004, 28

4 Kenny Cupers, *Housing Postwar France: The Social Project* (Minneapolis: University of Minnesota Press, 2014), xvi

5 Theresa Enright, *The Making of Grand Paris: Metropolitan Urbanism in the Twenty-first Century* (Cambridge: MIT Press, 2016), 8

6 The rapport Jean-Louis Borloo is the most recent official document, released in April 2018, deliberating on the social, cultural and economical disparities of the French society. http://www.cohesion-territoires.gouv.fr/IMG/pdf/sra4_complet.pdf Consulted on June 1st, 2018

7 Nicholas Sarkozy inaugurated the Grand Paris Project in 2007, and its many facets are currently unfolding in the metropolitan area. https://www.societedugrandparis.fr/gpe/le-grand-paris-express-en-resume, Consulted on June 7, 2018

8 Richard Klein, Gerard Hamel and Alex MacLean, *Les Grands Ensembles, Une Architecture du XXeme siecle* (Paris: Dominique Carré, 2011), 8.

9 A seminal issue of Project Urban, titled "Peripherie Maudite ou Splendide" gathers a series of point of views on the contrast between the center and peripheral zones. In particular, Manuel de Sola Morales' "La distance, Parametre majeure de la composition complex" is of interest here, "Peripherie maudite ou Splendide," *Project Urbain*, N8 Mai 1996, page 5,

10 Valérie Gaudard, Florence Margo-Schwoebel and Benoît Pouvreau, *1945-1975 Une histoire de l'habitat : 40 ensembles de logements "Patrimoine du XXe siècle,"* (Paris: Beaux Arts Editions, 2011)

11 Le Corbuiser refers to the ground as the Vegetable garden where the man/ snail will be finding his material and spiritual nourishments. Le Corbusier, *Athens Charter*.

PHANTOM MARKETS AND GHOST BOOTLEGGERS

STORYTELLING AS DESIGN

by LIZ TESTON

Spaces of interiority contain the stories we tell ourselves about our lives, our formative memories. The mind analyzes both new and frequented spaces in these terms, whenever we find places that seem familiar. The corners of our imagination fabricate phantom–buildings and ghost–companions. Our memories present themselves as we navigate the city. Through our senses and our memory-narratives, we understand the near environment. Phenomenology shapes the various places we frequent—our homes, marketplaces, the intimate recesses, and in-between-spaces of our cities. Although construction and renovation form new physical spaces, our memories remain.

This project explores alternative forms of design inquiry, seeking methods that emphasize the value of place in design. It investigates the different ways designers can engage with the near environment, to create subjective conditions of interiority in the urban exterior. An interior is not always circumscribed by the edges of a building. We can find conditions of interiority in many places—in isolated wooded areas, in exterior urban spaces, and in building interiors. This essay will uncover an alternative approach to the design process by reflecting on a recent oral history project.

The Knoxville Oral History Project aims to document the sensory experience of the long-demolished market-house in Knoxville, Tennessee. The multistory brick structure housed farmer's markets, a meeting hall, and other civic spaces. It burned in 1959 and was later demolished—leaving a void in the city grid.[1]

By re-appropriating techniques from other disciplines, this project defines new components of the design process. With the assistance of techniques like oral histories, designers can augment the pre-design phase, promoting a more phenomenologically detailed design that engages the essence of a community. This method acknowledges the perspective of all community members, longtime and short-lived. Careful observation and recognition of experiences and conditions steer the trajectory of a design proposal into a more inclusive, participatory design.

The city is an artifact.[2] If our imagination fabricates memory-based psychological interiorities, oral histories can also form collective, public interiorities. For instance, Ken Yates went square-dancing on the second floor of the market-house in Knoxville's Market Square. He was confronted by the police for public drunkenness in 1939. His bootlegger worked the southeast corner of Market

Ken Yates, Square-dancing with Bootleggers at the Market House. Collage by Linden Claytor. Historical image of the market house interior by McClung Historical Collection

Phantom Markethouse and contemporary Market Square. Collage by author.
Historical image of the market house by McClung Historical Collection

Street and Union Avenue. He told his story during his interview for the Knoxville Oral Histories Project, and we remember it whenever we pass the Market and Union crossroads. This happened eight decades ago. But, it is our collective memory now. These narratives become our realities, our psychological public interiorities. We see the ghost bootlegger on the corner. Through design and oral history, we can uncover the stories of our near environment.

This visual essay explores the interiority of our cities and our minds. Memories are the worthiest substance for a study of inhabited spaces, consciousness, and direct experience. Rising from these deep recesses, memory-narratives augment our understanding of place. The night insulates our reserve and emboldens us to explore the essence of intimacy. Collective memory influences these conditions of interiority, experienced by everyone that walks through Market Square. Our

perceptions and our memories tucked deep inside by day, are animated by the night. In the fullness of the evening's substance, we are carried back to the origin of our psyche, held close in a nearness and embraced by this interiority. We take refuge in the charcoal black. As Bachelard suggested, the evening holds an "intimate immensity," a vast heaviness so deep that it envelops the dreamer in familiarity.[3] That immensity, in turn, becomes a condition of interiority.

As an undergraduate, also around 1939, Gid Fryer and his fraternity brothers frequented downtown Knoxville in the evening. He said "Before the war, I was a fraternity man, in a drinking fraternity... after the war, I came back to the University with an entirely different approach to education...But, as an undergraduate, we were out for a good time, engaging in the sinful prac-tices of the city. On the west side of the Square or down Union Avenue, there was a hotel...the Service Hotel,

Ghost bootleggers at contemporary Market Square.
Collage and images by author

Gid Fryer, Fraternity brothers headed to the Standard Hotel. Collage by
Linden Claytor. Historical Image of Western Union Building by Thompson
Photograph Collection, McClung Historical Collection

She said "I liked to dress different. I wore [hot pants] a lot. Not to work, 'cause we had to have our pocketbooks match our shoes." Gail worked for the phone company, a place she described as wonderful. She went on to say "It was just a great place. I loved it. If I could go back in a past tense of my life, it wouldn't be my marriage, it would be my job. That's how much I loved it…It was a good job. I was good to the job. The job was good to me. If you were good to the job then the job would be good to you. If you put your heart into what you are doing, it is going to be good to you. I was a union spokeswoman. We'd walk picket lines. We'd stay out until we got what we wanted… But uh, it was just, I loved it. I loved getting off from work, meet my mom, we'd go shopping at Profit's, and Miller's. [Market Square] was just a wonderful place…"

Ken and Gail passed away within a week of each other, in July of 2017. Gid died in December of 2014.[4] The remains of Ken's bootlegger corner and Gail's hot pants store reveal memory-based interiorities. They demonstrate that the city reflects our essential selves. The parking lot where Gid's Union Avenue hotel once stood expresses the broad existential changes undergone in a lived-life. The city embodies these changes. The downtown building that houses Gail's phone company, for us, now symbolizes equal rights for women. Designers should collect narratives to uncover these psychological public interiorities.

Although demolition, construction, and renovation form new physical spaces, our memories remain consistent. Oral histories shape our perception of urban public interiority. By testing alternative forms of design inquiry, designers ask what methods can meaningfully communicate the qualities of place. How should designers best engage the character of a place in architectural design? Images and oral histories can reveal this character. Through this, we uncover an essential aspect of public interiority — the connectivity between memory and perception. This work will be used to inform future installations and interventions at Market Square as the project continues.

where subterranean parking is now. An open whore house, known [to all], you could visit the Service Hotel for whores." This story and these images materialize in the evening streets, creating an interior within the vastness of the city. The darkness folds Gideon's memories into our present-day, quotidian lives. These ghost-images evoke his youthful actions. They leave us wondering about the women from the Service Hotel and what they are doing today.

These conversations set out to uncover the experience of these unseen, ephemeral conditions. The interviewees included longtime Knoxville residents who had spent time in Market Square and the markethouse before it was demolished. They described the memories of their youth, events which would later be buried by the inhibitions and responsibilities of adulthood. These memories and events carry the dark bits that make up our essential selves. They form our perception of the near environment.

In the 1960s, Gail Wright shopped at Jilly's, a Market Square store depicted by Gail as a "wild dress shop."

ENDNOTES:

1 Jack Neely, *Market Square: A History of the Most Democratic Place on Earth*. (Knoxville: Market Square District Association, 2009), 12-14.

2 Aldo Rossi. *The Architecture of the City*. (Cambridge.: MIT Press, 1984), 20-28.

3 Gaston Bachelard, *The Poetics of Space*. (Boston: Beacon Street Press, 1969), 183-210.

4 Oral histories can be found at knoxhistories.org. Obituaries for Gid Fryer, Ken Yates, and Gail Wright can be found at http://jackneely.com/wordpress/2014/12/16/gideon-fryer-1921-2014/, https://tinyurl.com/yypo9kuk, and https://tinyurl.com/yxz5ktyo.

Gail Wright, Women in hot pants walking through Market Square. Collage by Linden Claytor. Historical Image of Market Square canopies by McClung Historical Collection

Temple of Saturn in Roman Forum, restored in late fourth century

RESTORATION IN HISTORICAL PERSPECTIVE

BETWEEN MEANING AND PRACTICE

by PHILIP JACKS

Although today there are commonly recognized boundaries between the practices of conservation, preservation and adaptive reuse, these terms have a relatively brief history. How that nomenclature came to be defined in our modern sense is at the intersection of architecture and science in the learned parlors of Paris during the first half of the nineteenth century. To understand the roots of those debates, however, we need to look more closely at the meaning of words in relation to building practice going back to classical antiquity.

In the political climate of France in the 1840s, when the restoration of the Madeleine at Vézelay and other Romanesque churches became a prerogative of Louis-Philippe's young administration, the concept of "restoration" carried nationalistic overtones. The suppression and vandalizing of abbeys and convents under Napoleon was of recent memory. To curb further ravages, the July Monarchy brought the safeguarding of monuments under control of the government.[1] Eugène Emmanuel Viollet-le-Duc spearheaded these efforts, notwithstanding his critics within the architectural profession, who had yet to agree upon a common set of guidelines or even the broader aims of historic preservation.

Viollet's entry on "*Restauration*" appeared in volume eight of the *Dictionnaire Raisonné* published in 1866. By then, he had been engaged with the Commission of Historic Monuments under the administration of Prosper Mérimée for over two decades.[2] Viollet begins with the premise that both the word and the idea (*le mot et la chose*) are modern figments and an historic anomaly. "*En effet aucune civilization, aucun peuple, dans les temps écoulés, n'a entendu faire des restaurations*

comme nous les comprenons aujourd'hui." This was more than just a mincing of words. Viollet's argument marked a radical shift from the nostalgic and Romantic appreciation of the medieval past, as vaunted in the writings of François Guizot and Jules Michelet, to a more rational approach based on the classifications used in scientific inquiry.[3] Viollet bolsters his position on philological grounds:[4]

> The Romans rebuilt; they did not restore. The proof of this is that there is not even a Latin word that corresponds to our word 'restoration' in the sense in which we understand the word today. *Instaurare, reficere, renovare* – none of these words means 'to restore' but rather 'to reestablish' or 'to rebuild anew.'

In classical literature, different words were used in different contexts: *renovo*, "to renew" or "replenish," generally in reference to pecuniary matters; *restituo*, more specifically about buildings.[5] In Suetonius, we read of Augustus's *restitutio* of his Palatine residence, of Nero's infamous Golden House rebuilt over the fire-ravaged Domus Transitoria (*incendio absumptam restitutamque*), and Vespasian leading the *restitutio* of the Capitoline by hauling off some of the burnt-out detritus on his head!

Inscriptions offered first-hand testimony, albeit fragmentary, but even here their interpretation is not always straightforward. A case in point is the Temple of Saturn, whose massive colonnade overlooks the southwest fringe of the Roman Forum. Its foundation is traditionally associated with Tarquinius Superbus around 497 B.C. That Republican temple was rebuilt anew and rededi-

cated by the Roman senator Munatius Plancus in 42 B.C., then destroyed by fire under the emperor Carinus in 283, then restored again in the late fourth century. This final reincarnation is recorded on the frieze: SENATVS POPVLVSQVE ROMANVS INCENDIO CONSVMPTVM RESTITVIT.[6] Renaissance architects, like Giovanni Antonio Dosio, could not fail to notice a short distance away the three solitary columns from the pronaos of the Temple of Titus and Vespasian, with a splinter of its frieze reading [R]ESTITUER[unt]. Its full inscription is known from the eighth-century Itinerarium by a monk from Einsiedeln – DIVO VESPASIANO AUGUSTO S.P.Q.R. IMP. CAES. SEVERUS ET ANTONINUS PII FELICES AUG. RESTITUER – which references both the later restorations under Severus and Caracalla, as well as the original founder. More curiously, given that the extant capitals, bases and entablature are entirely Flavian, archaeologists question what precisely was "restituted" in subsequent interventions?

In the high Latin of Augustan Rome, the verb *instaurare* usually referred to civic or religious rituals. In Virgil's *Aeneid* (IV, 63), Queen Dido desperately returns to the temple each day to renew her gift offerings and eventually receive the gods' countenance (*instauratque diem donis*). In another episode (IV, 145), Dionysus returns from India to his motherland in Greece and renews the ritual dances of his initiates (*instauratque choros*).[7] Livy speaks of the Roman armies, their general fallen, "renewing their combat afresh" against the Gauls (*novam de integro velle instaurare pugnam*).[8] Only once does Virgil infer a broader significance, in his recounting of the fall of Troy (II, 452): "*Instaurati animi regis succurrere tectis / auxilioque levare viros vimque addere victis*" ("Our spirits restored to succor the royal palace, to lift up and give life and vigor to the defeated men"). Aeneas,

with Anchises and Ascanius in tow, longs to bring back something irretrievably lost.

In the hands of Tacitus, a first century historian writing not of epic heroes but contemporary events, the substitution of *restaurare* for *instaurare* reflected how buildings bore the signs of political statecraft in imperial Rome. He notes how Marcus Lepidus asked leave from the Senate to renovate, at his own expense, the Basilica Aemilia in the Roman Forum founded by his ancestor Paulus Aemilius. Shortly after, Pompey's theater burnt down and Tiberius, finding none of Pompeius Magnus' descendants up to the task (*quod nemo e familia restaurando sufficeret*), undertook to rebuild it from the charred ruins himself. An emperor not known for his munificence, Tiberius again steps forward to restore the dilapidated temple of Venus on Mount Eryx in Sicily, moved by the supplications of the citizens of Segesta and claiming, as a member of the Julio-Claudian dynasty, to be descendant from the goddess.[9] In both instances, the act of *restauratio* could be seen as reaffirming an inheritance—whether to the posterity of the gens Pompeia, whose name Tiberius chose to preserve on the restored theater rather than his own; or to Aeneas, the mythical founder of Segesta, from whom the Iulii household traced their ancestry.[10]

Maurus Servius Honoratus, a grammarian living at the turn of the fourth century, is best known for his commentary on Virgil's writings. He likely held to polytheism, at a time when Rome's old religious institutions were giving way to Christianity. Though steeped in ancient sacred rites, Servius senses their passing. In a celebrated passage from the *Aeneid* (II, 15), Virgil recounts how the Greeks constructed the Trojan horse (*Instar montis equum divina Palladis arte*). Inexplicably, Servius

Giovan Antonio Dosio, Ruins of the Temple of Saturn and Temple of Vespasian in Roman Forum, c. 1540

Uffizi. Gabinetto dei Disegni, Florence, Arch. 2520r

digresses to the subject of architecture, inventing his own etymology by playing on the undeclined noun *instar* and the verb *instaurare*.[11]

> *Instar autem est ad similitudinem; unde non Restaurata, sed Instaurata dicuntur aedificia ad antiquam similitudinem facta.*

This might loosely be translated as: "A likeness, however, is [perceived] by resemblance, whence buildings made to resemble their old form are said to be not *restaurata*, but *instaurata*." Perhaps it is merely putting a fine point on grammatical usage; or perhaps Servius wished to differentiate between the restoring of temples and their wholesale despoiling, as older sancta were converted to new forms of worship. The phrase "*ad antiquam*" — we would say "the old-fashioned way" — exists only as an ideal, or memory. *Instauratio* becomes its representation in facsimile. To restore or to restitute, by contrast, is to be understood as process. It can never arrive at a replication of the original; it is always something other.[12]

Flavio Biondo's *De Roma Instaurata*, completed in 1446, offered the first comprehensive guidebook based on archaeological and topographical research. In the dedication to Eugenius IV, he presents his text as a surrogate for the physical form of the ancient city, which had been obliterated through barbarian invasions and the nefarious industry of medieval limekilns. Having earlier authored a treatise on spoken Latin, Biondo understood the gravity of words. He acknowledges the pope, whose returning of the Curia back to Rome (*conservatio*) gave impetus to his own literary reconstruction of its monuments (*instauratio Urbis*).[13] By the same token, Biondo is mindful not to vaunt his own creation over the actual rehabilitation underway: "…I would not contend that you, Eugenius, proceed to renew (*instaurare*) the monuments of Rome through my modest genius in letters as much you do by the labors being carried out by masons and carpenters."[14] Reading the ancient historian Cassiodorus, Biondo could hardly ignore the cannibalizing of antiquities sanctioned by later rulers from afar, notably the Ostrogothic king Theodoric, who in the fifth century permitted Romans to quarry from the Colosseum to repair the crumbling Aurelian walls around the city. Biondo condones this act (*in murorum illa instauratione funditus*), in mind of the fact that Theodoric, "an Arian and yet a Christian," put an end to the bloodsport of gladiators in the Flavian amphitheater.[15] Rather than a commemorative monument, Theodoric preferred to leave his stamp – REGNANTE D. N. THEODERICO FELIX ROMA — on thousands of bricks embedded in the city's ageing structures.[16]

In the famous Memorandum addressed to Leo X around 1517, Raphael and his collaborator Baldassare Castiglione laid out the progression of classical architecture from the early empire to their own day.

They single out the Arch of Constantine for its indiscriminate recycling of Hadrianic, Trajanic and Antonine reliefs — "maladroit (*alquanto goffo*), without art or any good design." At the same time, Raphael and Castiglione share an implicit understanding that the stock of Rome's ancient monuments, such as survived, had been "restored" repeatedly by successive emperors.

> "There is no need for anyone to question whether the less ancient of this era are lesser in beauty, less well conceived or of a different style. For they were all built in the same manner of beauty. And although many of the buildings were often restored (*ristaurati*) by the men of that age, as we may read that in the same place where the Golden House of Nero had stood the Baths of Titus and his House and the Amphitheatre were built, nevertheless these were constructed in the same style and manner *(con la medesima maniera e ragione)* as the other edifices of a time still older than the time of Nero and contemporary with the Golden House."[17]

Ironically, these were not "restorations" in any modern sense, but large-scale transformations leaving no trace of what had formerly stood on the site. In the case of the Domus Aurea, no sooner than Nero's name was extirpated from his monuments (*damnatio memoriae*), Galba hurriedly interred the coenatio and adjoining chambers on the Esquiline, on top of which Titus later erected his thermae. Similarly, Vespasian reclaimed the site of Nero's artificial lake (*stagnum*) for popular entertainments in the Flavian Amphitheater. *Maniera and ragione*, then, referred strictly to the technical art of construction. An assiduous reader of Vitruvius, Raphael had studied examples of opus lateritium, opus quadratum and opus reticulatum and experimented with these techniques in his own projects, notably the Villa Madama.

Raphael, whom the pope had appointed as Commissariat for the protection of ancient marbles from unscrupulous privateers, held a special reverence for the Pantheon. Although it had been rededicated to Santa Maria ad Omnes Martyres centuries earlier, Raphael's desire to be buried in one of its niches was most unusual. According to Vasari, the artist arranged at great cost for one of the ancient tabernacles to be "restored… using new stones" (*si restaurasse… di pietre nuove*) and a marble statue of the Madonna placed over his tomb.[18] Like Raphael, Vasari understood the act of restoration as integrating new elements into the existing niche, while preserving its stylistic unity (*buon stile antico*). Ultimately, their concept of rebirth (*rinascita*) rested on the belief in an historical continuum from antiquity to their own day, broken only by the interlude of foreign incursions. It was predicated on a set of common morphologies, notably the classical orders, and put into practice by imitating from a canon of exempla. As such, it ended with the Renaissance. "From the seventeenth century, resemblance was pushed out to the boundaries of knowledge," notes Michel Foucault, to be supplanted by a new epistemological system "according to the forms of identity, of difference, and of order."[19] In distancing themselves from the past and adopting an historicist view, later philologists also rejected the neologism "*restauratio*" as a corruption of classical Latin. In 1722 Johannes Vorst, cited the word for censure in his *De latinitate falso suspecta*, observing that what Germans understood by "*wiederbauen*" was properly translated as *instaurare*.[20] John Hill, in a discourse to the Royal Society of Edinburgh in 1786, observed that the verb *restaurare* "rests upon authority that is not to be trusted," while *instaurare* is employed among the "purer writers."[21]

In their famous debate of 1830, Etienne Geoffroy Saint-Hilaire and Georges Cuvier excited public audiences with a new method of scientific inquiry. While their conclusions differed radically, their method had ramifications across a wide range of fields. What it offered to the study of historic monuments was a new way of analyzing not just what remained but what no longer existed – "the emergence of 'resemblances' where there is no 'identical' element," notes Foucault, "a resemblance that is constituted by the transition of the function into evident invisibility."[22] Organisms identified and classified by function had their counterparts in the working components of building systems. For Viollet-le-Duc, it was the beginning of a new era and there was no turning back:

> Cuvier, by means of his studies of comparative anatomy, as well as of his geologic research, unveiled to the public almost literally from one day to the next a very long history of the world that had preceded the reign of mankind. People were captivated by Cuvier's revelations and eager to travel down the new path he had charted for them.[23]

In the *Leçons d'anatomie comparé*, first published in 1802, Cuvier demonstrated how an entire organism could be recovered from a fragmentary fossil. Both Cuvier and his arch-rival Geoffroy recognized the immediacy of their findings to the classifying of human habitation and even the growth of cities.[24] Cuvier had collaborated in 1806 with Alexandre Brongniart, eponymous son of the famous architect, on a geological survey of Paris and its environs. Cuvier imagined a scope to his work well beyond the natural sciences, as he professed in the *Preliminary Discourse*:[25]

> I am trying to make known the neglected monuments of the history of the earth. I am an antiquary of a new kind. I have had to learn how to decipher and to restore these monuments, how to recognize and reassemble their scattered and mutilated fragments from their fragments in their original order...

From here, it was but a small step to reconstructing

Romanesque and Gothic churches down to their smallest detail by extrapolating from surviving fragments. Gottfried Semper, living in Paris at the time, recalled years later visiting the Jardin des Plantes, where he inspected Cuvier's "fossil remains of the animal tribes of the primeval world" laid out in a long series. The display inspired him to devise his own comparative system of architectural types classified by material over three millennia.[26]

Cuvier and Geoffroy diverged on the question of whether over time species could adapt and transform themselves to changes in habitat. This was a point of special relevance to the circle of Léon Vaudoyer, Léonce Reynaud and Henri Labrouste. Whereas Cuvier could not accept the premise of evolution, specifically the mutability of organisms, these architects grasped on to the theory of "adaptionism," as in the case of the Greek temples of Sicily, whose design was determined by the conditions of climate, site and materials at a precise historical moment. To properly reconstruct their forms, they maintained, one would need to recreate those environmental factors and not merely reproduce "an historical vignette."[27]

Semper never accepted "natural selection" as a viable explanation for the development of architectural form, though he conceded that one could rightly regard "old monuments as the fossilized receptacles (*Gehäuse*) of extinct social organizations."[28] Similarly, it is a stretch to say that Viollet, writing several years after the publication of Darwin's *On the Origin of Species* (1859), subscribed to an evolutionary theory with respect to the progression of architectural styles through time. And he had little patience for men like Labrouste and other pensionnaires who theorized from a "dream world" at the French Academy in Rome, far removed from actual conditions on the ground. Rather, Viollet saw the work of the restorer in clinical terms, referring to medieval structures as "delicate organisms."[29] Indeed, he may be accused of tampering with the natural order of "survival of the fittest" by introducing modern materials, notably cast and wrought iron, to improve the structural efficiency of Gothic monuments. "The restored building needs to be given a longer lease on life than the one that is near expiration."[30] In the sweeping urban reform of Paris directed by Baron Haussmann, adaptive reuse, whatever one might have called it, was preferable to the more common alternative of demolition.[31]

> The fact is that the best of all ways of preserving a building is to find a use for it, and then to satisfy so well the needs dictated by that use that there will never be any further need to make any further changes in the building.

Viollet would have lamented the fate of the Petits Augustins, removed from their convent in 1795, which then served as the Musée des Monuments Français

OPPOSITE TOP
Alò Giovannoli, Engraving of the ruins of the Thermae Titi on the Esquiline, *Vedute degli antichi vestigj di Roma...* **(Rome, 1616), fol. 81r.**

LEFT

Refectory of the priory of Saint-Martin-des-Champs, Paris

Engraving by Lemaitre from France, *L'Univers pittoresque, deuxieme partie*, published by Firmin Didot Frères, Paris, 1845

RIGHT

Library of the Conservatoire des Arts et Métiers, as restored from the refectory of Saint-Martin-des-Champs by Vaudoyer.

Engraving by C. W. Sheeres after E. Shirond, 1857

until 1820, when given over to the École des Beaux-Arts. François Debret turned the cloister into an historical pastiche, mostly Italian Renaissance in spirit, redubbed the Bâtiment des Loges, for which he was harshly criticized.[32] By contrast, Viollet gave a back-handed compliment to Vaudoyer – though he does not mention his name – as the architect charged with renovating the refectory of St.-Martin-des-Champs as a library for the Conservatoire des Arts et Métiers. From 1845 to 1849, Vaudoyer dismantled the walls, columns and vaults of the thirteenth-century building, stone by stone, then reassembled its components, in some cases adding modern materials, such as iron frames for the lancet windows and a sub-floor for gas heating. Viollet insisted, wherever possible, on respecting the structural rationale of the medieval builder. Similarly, Vaudoyer had immured openings surfaced in stucco with faux masonry and painted to simulate the structural system of ribs and infill vaults. Even the Gothic bookcases and long tables arrayed down the center were intended to recreate the aura of a spiritual repast, only now instead of monks, scientists would congregate for their animated soirées.[33] The architect in question, notes Viollet, "if he was going to respect the construction at the same time as he was restoring it, had to organize the bookshelves and compartments in such a way that there would never again be any neces-

sity to alter the dispositions of the room." [34] For Viollet, in the end, there was only informed and uninformed stewardship, regardless of whether buildings had outgrown their original program. To faithfully restore historical monuments, the architect's most solemn task was not to imitate the past, but to divine its generative spirit.

ENDNOTES:

1 Kevin D. Murphy, *Memory and Modernity: Viollet-le-Duc at Vézelay* (Pennsylvania State University Press, University Park: 2000), pp. 40–41.

2 *Dictionnaire Raisonné de l'Architecture française du XIe au XVIe Siècle par M. Viollet-le-Duc, Architecte du Gouvernement Inspecteur-Général des Edifices Diocésains* (Paris: A. Morel & C. éditeurs, 1875), tom. VIII, pp. 14–34. 6

3 Eugène-Emmanuel Viollet-le-Duc, *The Foundations of Architecture. Selections from the Dictionnaire raisonné*, introduction by Barry Bergdoll, translation by Kenneth D. Whitehead (New York, George Braziller: 1990), p. 6.

4 *Dictionnaire raisonné*, op. cit., p. 196.

5 Cicero, *Oratio in Verrem* I, 4, 11, rebukes Verres for despoiling homes and temples while serving as legate of Asia and

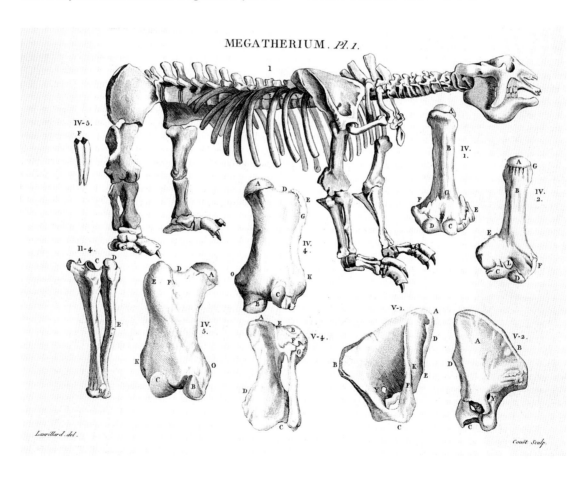

MEGATHERIUM. *Pl. 1.*

Georges Cuvier, *Recherches sur les ossemens fossils* (Paris, 1812), Elephans section, Megatherium (Giant Sloth)

Pamphylia, repeating the infamous acts during his previous tenure as quaestor (*suum scelus illus pristinum renovavit et instauravit quaestorium*).

6 Filippo Coarelli, "Aedes Saturni," in *Lexicon Topographicum Urbis Romae*, vol. IV, ed. Eva Margareta Steinby (Edizioni Quasar, Rome: 1999), pp. 234–235.

7 *The Fourth Book of Virgil's Aeneid on the Loves of Dido and Aeneas*, ed. Richard Fanshawe (Basil Blackwood, London: 1935), p. 23.

8 Virgil, *Aeneid* X, 543. Livy, *Ab urbe condita* X, 29; again in XXXVII, 19.

9 Tacitus, *Annalium* IV, 43: "...et Segestani aedem Veneris montem apud Erycum, vetustate dilapsam, restaurari postulavere, nota memorantes de origine eius et laeta Tiberio, suscepit cuam libens ut consanguineo."

10 Cornelius Tacitus, *Annalium* IV, 43, ed. H. Furneaux (Oxford, Clarendon Press: 1889), p. 368.

11 Wilfred P. Mustard, "The Etymologies in the Servian Commentary to Vergil," *Colorado College Studies* III (1892): 23–24, notes *instaurare* may be cognate with *instar*, but is hardly derived from it. See D. du Cange, *Glossarium mediae et infimae latinitatis*, tom. VII (Paris: Librairie des sciences et des arts, 1938), p. 154.

12 See Philip Jacks, "Restauratio and Reuse: The Afterlife of Roman Ruins," *Places: Forum of Design for the Public Realm*, vol. 20, no. 1 (Summer 2008), 11f.

13 Blondi Flavij Forliviensis, *De Roma Instaurata* libri tres (Impressit Bernardinus Sylva, 1527), fol. ii

14 Ibid. "...ego omnia quae mihi adsunt tuae scientati debeo, cur & non ipse contendam: ut sic tu Romam per ingenioli mei litterarum monumenta, sicuti cementariorum fabrorumque lignariorum opera peragis instaurare."

15 Biondo, *De Roma instaurata* III, 6, citing from Cassiodorus, *Variae* III, 49.

16 See further, Biondo Flavio, *Romae Triumphantis libri decem*, II, 33, Latin text ed. Maria Agata Pincelli, intro. and translation Frances Muecke (Harvard University Press, Cambridge-London: 2016), pp. 240–41. Rodolfo Lanciani, *The Destruction of Ancient Rome* (Benjamin Blom, New York: 1901), p. 78: "I have never made or witnessed an excavation on the site of any of the great buildings of Rome without discovering one or more of Theodoric's bricks."

17 "A Report to Pope Leo X on Ancient Rome," translated in *A Documentary History of Art, vol. I. The Middle Ages and the Renaissance*, ed. Elizabeth Gilmore Holt (Doubleday Anchor, New York: 1973), pp. 293-94.

18 David Karmon, *The Ruin of the Eternal City: Antiquity and Preservation in Renaissance Rome* (Oxford University Press, New York: 2011), p. 160. See Vincenzo Golzio, *Raffaello nei documenti, nelle testimonianze dei contemporanei e nella letteratura del suo secolo* (Vatican City, Panetto & Petrelli: 1936), p. 229.

19 Michel Foucault, *The Order of Things*. An Archaeology of the Human Sciences, trans. from *Les Mots et Les Choses* (New York, Random House: 1970), p. 71.

20 Johannes Vorst, *De latinitate falso suspecta, deque Latinae linguae cum germanica convenientia liber* (Leipzig, ex Officina Thomae Fritschii: 1722), p. 138.

21 "An Essay upon the Principles of Historical Composition, with an Application of those Principles to the Writings of Tacitus," in *Transactions of the Royal Society of Edinburgh*, vol. I (London, J. Dickson: 1788), p. 196. Alexander Crombie, in his *Gymnasia, sive Symbola Critica* (London, J. Johnson: 1812), vol. I, p. 119 called the word a "superfluous, and blameable innovation," while conceding its widespread reception in later centuries.

22 Foucault, *The Order of Things*, ed. cit., p. 264.

23 *Dictionnaire raisonné*, ed. cit.,

24 Paula Young Lee, "The meaning of molluscs: Leonce Reynaud and the Cuvier-Geoffroy Debate of 1830, Paris," in *Narrating Architecture: A Retrospective Anthology*, ed. James Madge and Andrew Peckham (Routledge, London-New York: 2006), pp. 140–42. The "Maison de Cuvier," whose rooms had grown like an unseemly organism from one to three stories, appeared to some Parisians like a nautilus – in the class of mollusques, alongside the zoophytes, arthropods and vertebrates.

25 *Discours préliminaire sur les revolutions du globe* (1812), cited in Dorinda Outram, George Cuvier: *Vocation, science and authority in post-revolutionary France* (Manchester, Manchester University Press: 1984), p. 151.

26 For Semper's initial essay, "Entwurf eines Systemes der vergleichenden Stillehre," see Ute Poerschke, *Architectural Theory of Modernism: Relating Functions and Forms* (Routledge, New York and London: 2016), pp. 75–78. Mari Hvattum, *Gottfried Semper and the Problem of Historicism* (Cambridge University Press, 2004), 127–130. For a more nuanced assessment of Cuvier's influence, cf. Harry Francis Mallgrave, *Gottfried Semper: Architect of the Nineteenth Century* (New Haven & London, Yale University Press: 1996), 157f.

27 Caroline van Eck, "What was Revolutionary about the Romantic Pensionnaires: The role of biology in the work of Labrouste, Vaudoyer, and Renaud," in *L'architecture, les sciences et la culture de l'histoire au XIXe siècle* (Publications de l'Université de Saint-Etienne, 2001), 83–98.

28 See Harry Francis Mallgraves' introduction to Gottfried Semper, *Style in the Technical and Tectonic Arts*; or, *Practical Aesthetics*, trans. Harry Francis Mallgrave and Michael Robinson (Getty Research Institute, Los Angeles: 2004), pp. 53, 57, n. 38.

29 *Dictionnaire raisonné*, ed. cit., p. 224.

30 *Dictionnaire raisonné*, ed. cit., p. 214.

31 *Dictionnaire raisonné*, ed. cit., p. 222.

32 On the critique of Théophile Thoré, see David Van Zanten, *Designing Paris: The Architecture of Duban, Labrouste, Duc, and Vaudoyer* (MIT Press, Cambridge-London: 1987), p. 67.

33 Barry Bergdoll, *Léon Vaudoyer: Historicism in the Age of Industry* (Architectural History Foundation, MIT Press, Cambridge-London: 1994), pp. 165–67.

34 *Dictionnaire raisonné*, ed. cit.

**Thomas Wilder, 2018, 42" Inkjet print placed atop the subject matter
of the image**

INVESTIGATIONS: BETWIXT AND BETWEEN

by ANNE WEST

In all our voluntary thinking there is some topic or subject about which all the members of the thought revolve. Half the time this topic is a problem, a gap we cannot yet fill with a definite picture, word, or phrase, but which... influences us in an intensely active and determinate psychic way. Whatever may be the images and phrases that pass before us, we feel their relation to this aching gap. To fill it up is our thoughts' destiny. Some bring us nearer to that consummation. Some the gap negates as quite irrelevant. Each swims in a felt fringe of relations of which the aforesaid gap is the term.[1]

— William James

I'd like to offer myself as witness to a process in which a group of graduate students at Rhode Island School of Design pursued explorations of "the space between" in my seminar *Investigations: Betwixt and Between*. All entered this class knowing that the nature of this space was worthy of examination; that it could serve and nourish their practice as a zone for inquiry, inspiration, and translation. Through a close review of a repertoire of readings, and through sustained, facilitated interaction in writing and discussion, the class became a direct opportunity to deepen reflection and to integrate a personal perspective on the character of this space.

On an intellectual and emotional level, an exploration of the between is an abstract and mysterious process, yet on a formal level, it presents an opportunity for concrete and precise action. What follows are principles of inflection that map a pedagogy. I've structured these writings to include a concise view of students' process to show how they consider various forms, states, and contexts of the between.

Such a pedagogy is not merely a method; rather it is a path to awareness or, as architect and educator David Gersten points out, to spatial literacy: "There is no architecture without the humanities, there is no space without breath, voice, poetry."[2] It has far greater power expressed through the cultivation of perceptions, attitudes, and interventions that are necessary to work effectively as a practitioner in the space between. What I observed in this community of inquiry, both in discussion and as the students read aloud their insights at the end of the seminar, was straight-ahead clarity for what matters for living in a habitable world.

I
THE GAP
One must listen to space.
We gather a glimpse of what is experienced and absorbed through this practice of exploring the unscripted gap as Thomas Wilder, a graduate student in photography (MFA 2020), comes into attunement with the identity of a site: his studio space. For Wilder, this inherited workspace becomes a light- and texturally-sensitive surface upon which, and through which, he locates himself in the gap between perceiving and knowing. Through close inhabitation, and through the development and replication of images and gestures, he reveals what is latent in the myriad particularities of the studio. A path of light caused by the artificial light from surrounding buildings comes to life, as both phenomena and document, after dark. A palimpsest of scuff marks tracking movement across the threshold returns to the threshold as a single image.

Wilder brings to awareness multiple thought processes subtly archived in the walls: an index of intentional, shifting or misplaced calculations as previous artists worked out the display of their work for review. These spectral presences come into visibility as singular moments yet also in indeterminate replications in space intimately connecting us to undocumented narratives. In the art of photography, aren't all images evidence of transient phenomena stilled through exposure? Wilder's insertion in space as an observer involves a temporality in *medias res*. And, as he comes into relation with the experience of presence and absence, we discover through the traces, a new composition emerging in the gap. Here the potential of his work links us to a fresh perception of space as an interval in the flow of both light and shadow.

II
A LIMINAL CONDITION
It inspires us to a great sense of care and responsibility toward self and others.
Cultural anthropologist Victor Turner's "communitas"[3] and physicist David Bohm's articulation of dialogue[4] helped graphic designer Elaine Lopez (MFA, 2019) uncover the driving force behind her empathic design practice.

A brief synopsis of the writings of Turner and Bohm may help to provide context for an understanding of Lopez's work on human interaction.

LEFT
Thomas Wilder, 2018, 21" Inkjet print displayed with lights off

RIGHT
Thomas Wilder, 2018, 21" Inkjet print displayed with lights on

Victor Turner offers a perspective on the "between" as a liminal condition — a real or symbolic threshold. It is a space in which society can take cognizance of itself. To enter this space requires a break from structure and a stripping away of hierarchies. When under this condition, one can never be too parochial as it alters understanding in relation to others, place and time, which in turn feeds the spirit of *communitas* or social interrelatedness. Turner asserts that cultures suffer without *communitas*; this time without structure nurtures the potential for a higher pitch of self and social consciousness.

David Bohm adds to an understanding of the potential of the space between as one for dialogue (*dia*—through and *logos*—meaning of the word). Dialogue, in the Bohmian sense, is a free-flowing stream of meaning between individuals, which in turn leads to a broader understanding. As we grow beyond our tendency toward proclamation, through practices of deep listening to one another and in an authentic exchange with our curiosities and the deeper questions in our hearts, we become changed. New potential for communication opens, which in turn leads to community.

In her project, *Hot Air*, Lopez uses the platform of design to highlight these relational concerns, asking us to look at the tense boundaries that emerge when competition defines an encounter rather than dialogue. Framed as an interactive workshop, two participants are invited to select balloons of their choosing and to insert and inflate them in a transparent, acrylic box. Each balloon, marked by a specific color, becomes a character

in the scenario. As each balloon grows in size within an individualistic power play, the participants become obscured from sight. The dynamic ends when one balloon bursts. In this non-dialogic space, no one sees the other, no one is listening.

Since the emphasis of her work is on building conditions for empathy with perspectives other than our own, dialogue is essential. Lopez understands (and asserts through her work) the importance of keeping access between individuals open, which involves a constant inner and outer motion of building connection through awareness of another's condition. In the free-flowing stream of meaning in the space between, *communitas* becomes possible.

III
DOUBLENESS
Introducing into play the duality of the liminal condition coaxes the living tension alive in the work.
One of the exercises that I give the students is to explore the double nature of their work. According to French anthropologist Claude Levi-Strauss, things that matter happen along binary lines.[5] In other words, everything has a built-in dichotomy. Familiar to our daily life are dualities such as night and day, moist and dry, open and hidden, order and chaos, for example. In one of our writing exercises, we record the binary pairings that appear in the work and then we move toward an understanding of how they play out as a discernible design language.

Anna Albrecht, a graduate student in Interior Architecture (MDes, 2019) discovered her design process

Elaine Lopez and Adam Chuong, *Hot Air*, 2018 (screen shots from video), Clear acrylic, silver tape, latex balloons, 15 x 15 x 15"

Anna Albrecht, *Super[structure]*, Monongahela National Forest, Webs, 2018

in the between. With an eye to her graduate thesis, she had for some time felt an inexplicable draw to a series of abandoned fire stations in the Allegheny Mountain region of West Virginia. These towers, which she refers to as "super-terrestrials," are set deep in the Monongahela National Forest, requiring on-foot access. Her desire was to develop a spatial design that realized her infrastructural dream of bringing reliable broadband internet to people of this region.

Despite a restless nudge over several months, she was unable to lay down the conceptual particulars of a design scheme. A reservoir of understanding emerged for Albrecht when she was asked to investigate the double nature of these towers. Only by paying attention to the paradoxes expressed in their pronounced verticality, uncanny form, materiality, and location did the unique character of this site come forward. Exploring the liminal condition of these towers opened awareness to the contradictory imperatives expressed between lightness and solidity, earth and sky, mundane and sacred, progress and wildness, connected and empty, grounded and sublime.

The towers have a web-like structure with ample negative space, yet they are also massively solid, weighing between 6,000 to 18,000 pounds. They are set deep within the forest, yet pierce the tree canopy reaching into the open sky with generous panoramic views. From a "both and" perspective, her design invites trekkers to

hike to a tower for a private sleeping quarter. Yet in this silent refuge in nature, they find the terms of *communitas* both through communal internet and the infinity of the night sky. As Albrecht writes, "Trekkers who undertake this route, while walking for their own reasons, will come upon a tower after a day of private rumination, only to become overcome with a sense of wonder."[6] From this elevated platform, one is launched into the silent, deep space of darkness.

IV
THRESHOLDS OF THE BETWEEN
Liminality is a threshold condition.
Whether outside looking in or inside looking out, the condition of the threshold involves complex connections with space and phenomena where specific qualities of material, light difference, and elements of time come into play.

Interior Architecture graduate Rhea Roy Thomas (MA, 2019) maintains that to consider the threshold from the perspective of architecture adds meaning to movement as well as clarity to how spaces should be interpreted and used. In exploring numerous variations of threshold forms, Thomas was able to understand ways of linking and separating spaces, mediating movement from very public to private. In assessing the movement from one spatial status to another, she explored how interior worlds associate and open to adjacencies

A *Jaali* wall at the Amer Fort, located in the city of Jaipur, Rajasthan, India

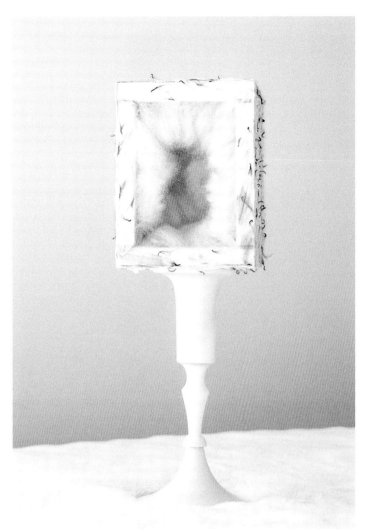

affecting user experience. Defining elements such as doors, arches, dividing walls, columns, and screens were considered, as well as degrees of opacity and position. For example, with a more opaque threshold, comes a more abrupt transition. Open thresholds with more ambiguous boundaries allow a free-flowing movement.

Highlighted in her study, as a strong example of threshold form, is *jaali* (meaning "net" in Hindi) which appears in Indian architecture. According to Thomas, *jaali* decoration allows both privacy and publicness. With many small perforations in a stone wall or as latticed screen, a boundary is created that gives interiority an external presence by allowing eternal elements of light and heat to pass through. Through *jaali* holes from within, everything outside is visible, but from the outside, nothing is visible due to the light difference. The cuts reduce the glare but allow for illumination, without affecting the intensity of the light. These walls or screens provide varying degrees of transparency and opacity and are climatologically suitable for the hot and humid Indian climate. In Thomas's words, "*Jaali* achieved the glamor of glass with an uninterrupted view with aesthetic grace as well as environmental manage-ment—all within socio-cultural denominations of privacy and security."[7]

V
BECOMING THRESHOLD
It opens us to something immeasurable, to what may exist outside human knowledge.
A threshold represents a transitional passage, moving from one state to another. It is neither here nor there. What is known falls behind as we go beyond a previous order, into a new perspective, a new structure of

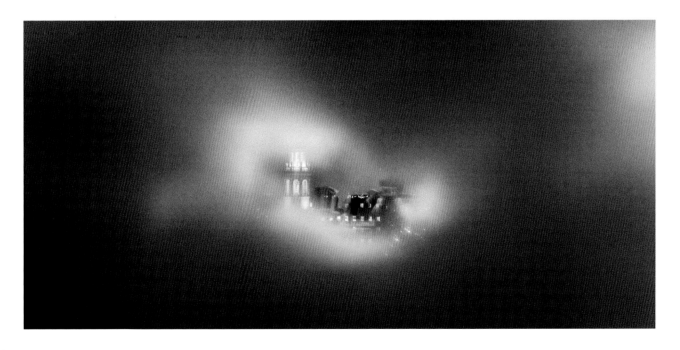

TOP
Zhiqing Guo, *Senseutopia*, **2019,**
Daisy petals, wool felt, canvas petals,
candlestick

BOTTOM
Zhiqing Guo, *Senseutopia*, **2019,**
Digital photograph

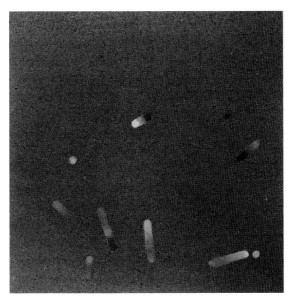
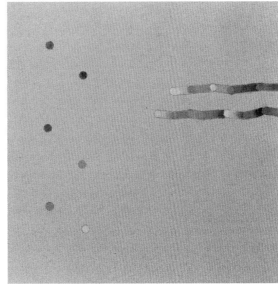

thought, a new process perhaps. It is important to note that our emotional and perceptual interactions during this liminal state have a precise form of understanding; they carry a level of depth.

With her focal device *Senseutopia*, 2019, Jewelry and Metals student Zhiqing Guo (MFA, 2019) asks us to become aware of her felt experience of seeing. With this device, she engages with the psychological and poetic inflections that emerge between self and space as we look into the boundless emptiness of sky. In this limbo state, there is only the subtle play of light that activates a sight threshold. Devoid of gravity, yet tethered to the intimacy of the body, we see augmented transparency, holding empty air. And it is precisely in this emergence of awareness that Guo understands that she is in a state of being within exteriority. Through the sensing bridge of her device, we are given a sublime launch into reverie. Boundaries become porous.

"My work is born in an invisible between space — a placeless place that offers itself as a translucent layer of the space in which I live. It seems true somehow as it appears in front of my eyes but then disappears. Always fleeting, I do not have enough time to perceive it or even to speak out...The space I am trying to articulate is the most familiar unknown. It's evanescent with an unstable sensuous boundary. That familiar unknown space is the presence in my work."[8]

Conclusion

To occupy "the space between" demands a perceptual orientation where we pay close attention to the spatial environment and to the relational nature of experience. We are present in our perceptions and in our lives fully as we become alert to what are we opening into. The transformations that we generate in the work — whether an object, architecture, or design initiative — we also generate in ourselves. It is this deeper responsiveness and sensitivity within the liminal condition that is, in fact, fundamental to our humanity. To reach an understanding of this condition means becoming liminal ourselves.

Gonzalo Nuñez Galetto (MFA, 2020) offers this reflective summary:

"It's a fluid, adaptive process of continually emptying out, responding to conditions, and coming into collaborative participation with others that invites listening, observing, and intuiting in different directions...The complexity for interaction and possibility for complication grow even larger when one considers living environments and the diverse forms of sentient life that also occupy these spaces."[9]

ENDNOTES:

1 From William James, *The Principles of Psychology, Vol. 1* (New York: Henry Holt, 1890), as quotes in Laing, Katherine Knight, 259.

2 David Gersten, email message to author, February 10, 2019.

3 Victor Turner. *Dramas, Fields, and Metaphors: Symbolic Action in Human Society,* Cornell University Press, 1975, 231-271.

4 David Bohm. *On Dialogue,* Routledge, 2014.

5 Claude Levi-Strauss, *The Raw and the Cooked,* trans. John and Doreen Weightman (New York: Harper & Row, 1969). Levi-Strauss extended the ideas of binary pairings to anthropology, in such oppositions as nature/culture, raw/cooked, inedible/edible.

6 From class writing exercise, Anna Albrecht, RISD, 2019.

7 From class writing exercise, Rhea Roy Thomas, RISD, 2019.

8 From class writing exercise, Zhiqing Guo, RISD, 2019.

9 From class writing exercise, Gonzalo Nuñez Galetto, RISD, 2019.

LEFT

Gonzalo Nuñez Galetto, *Transmission*
#14, 2015, Acrylic and oil on wood panel
9 X 9 inches

RIGHT

Gonzalo Nuñez Galetto , *Transmission*
#19, 2015, Acrylic and oil on wood panel
9 X 9 inches

ABSENT MATTER

AN INTERVIEW WITH EDOARDO TRESOLDI

by LILIANE WONG

In 2016, Italian artist Edoardo Tresoldi constructed a monumental wire mesh installation at the archaeological park of Siponto, in the southern Italian region of Puglia. Abandoned in the 13th century, the site includes fragments of Apulian-Romanesque architecture and the remains of a Paleo–Christian Basilica. 'Basilica di Siponto' offered a contemporary interpretation/re–interpretation of the basilica that earned Tresoldi worldwide acclaim. The installation also served as a new provocation for innovative approaches to preservation and heritage. In 2018, Tresoldi was awarded the 'Gold Medal for Italian Architecture — Special Prize to Commission' by the Triennale di Milano for this bold and visionary intervention that crosses and connects disciplines from sculpture and preservation to public art. Tresoldi has since engaged in new projects that further probe complex issues of intervention and site, not only in Italy but in cities around the world from France to Spain and from the USA to the United Arabic Emirates. He shares his thoughts with Int|AR on his path to Siponto, new work in Paris and Rome, explorations of material and investigations beyond time and space, all of which offer us thoughtful and insightful new views of adaptive reuse. In "Absent Matter," Edoardo Tresoldi takes us on a journey in which "places, instants and beings are narrated."

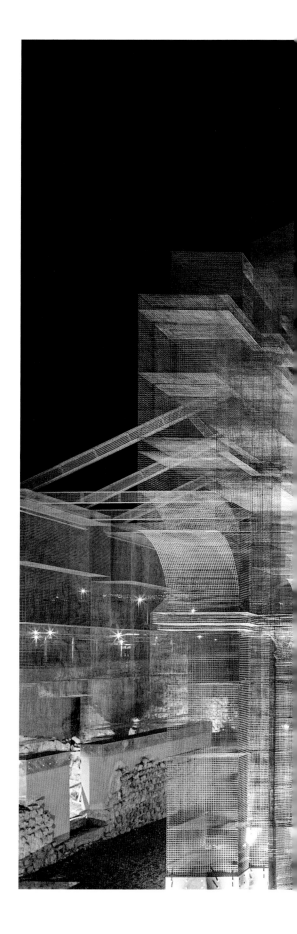

Basilica Di Siponto, a permanent installation commissioned by the Ministry
of Cultural Heritage and Activities and Tourism, Manfredonia, Italy, 2016

Int|AR: You operate in between numerous and varied dimensions: time & space, art & archaeology, classical and modern, place & absence, limits & the unbound. With a background in fields including cinema, music, and sculpture, can you speak to the influence of these many creative areas on your heterogeneous vision of art?

ET: I come from the world of cinema, where I worked as a scenographer for 7 years. So yes, it certainly had an influence on my next career, especially in composition and in a spirit of cinematographic "framing" that pushes me to immediately consider how a work will be reproduced.

I have many musician friends with whom I have several projects in the pipeline. We spend hours in my Milan studio experimenting and discussing how music's creative process can be adapted to that of sculpture—after all they are structured in the same area of the brain—and how music and sculpture can strike similar chords.

What we find most stimulating is not so much an understanding of how to combine them, but rather how a musician designs architecture, how an architect composes a song or how a musician sculpts.

Int|AR: The Int|AR Journal focuses on the subject of adaptive reuse, defined as the practice of giving new purpose to existing structures. Our exploration of this subject has, at times, been analogized to the idea of palimpsest such that different architectural interventions in existing context are viewed as adding layers in time. In your projects involving heritage structures such as the Archaeological Park of Siponto, what type of layer would you term your interventions of wire mesh forms?

ET: They certainly belong to the contemporary, to the present. The ephemeral is an essential aspect in my poetry and my work. The *Basilica of Siponto* project, for example, was designed to "exist" for several years, but with no claim to impose itself on subsequent

ABOVE AND OPPOSITE
Aura, a temporary installation at the Le Bon Marché Rive Gauche, Paris, France, 2017

Aura, a temporary installation at the Le Bon Marché Rive Gauche, Paris, France, 2017

generations. I believe it is necessary to respect unequivocally the place and the passage of time.

In general, my interventions are based on the temporal existence of a place; their duration depends on the type of project, the place, the purpose and the type of narration.

Int|AR: Your work is achieved primarily through the use of a single material: wire mesh. And you speak of it as 'absent matter'. How and why did you choose this material? Were you working with other materials before focusing on wire mesh?

ET: I have been drawing since I was 5 and for my entire career I have been in contact with materials of differing nature and characteristic.

I discovered wire mesh when I was a scenographer and was immediately struck by its potential to convey a light and subtle tale that could merge with the surrounding environment. I started with figurative sculptures, and then delved into the architectural realm.

Int|AR: The project at the Archaeological Park of Siponto is premised upon the remains of the Paleo Christian Basilica. It is a novel direction in working with history, heritage and legacy. How does your intervention relate to the ruins? To the remaining Romanesque church?

ET: First, I studied the historical documentation with a team of archaeologists and researchers. Gradually I realized that I had to suggest the reappearance of the Basilica, not by faithfully reconstructing it, but redesigning it in the air according to its own language. It is important for me to generate an intervention that does not require any specific knowledge to be fully accessed and assimilated.

I then tried to make the emotional and physical aspects of that place my own; I considered it as a character and outlined the narrative elements. Starting from the identification of the lines that recall the original identity, I worked on the morphology to give life to architectural echoes and tensions that relate to the landscape

Basilica Di Siponto, a permanent installation commissioned by the Ministry of Cultural Heritage and Activities and Tourism, Manfredonia, Italy, 2016

Basilica Di Siponto, a permanent installation commissioned by the Ministry
of Cultural Heritage and Activities and Tourism, Manfredonia, Italy, 2016

through transparency: the tree, as well as the conformation of the landscape and the Romanesque church have become fundamental elements in the design phase.

Int|AR: Would you categorize your work in what is today sometimes termed 'experimental preservation'?

ET: I would define it more as dynamic conservation: intervening in an archaeological site allowed me to build a contemporary landmark, able to dialogue with the pre-existing in a new way. Siponto has turned out to be a cultural operation in which art, landscape, history and the environment merge through a strongly empathetic interpretation with regard to visitors.

Int|AR: The term 'ghostly' is often used to describe your work. Is this an accurate description? How does such an adjective apply to heritage and ruins?

ET: It is. The 'Absent Matter', narrated through the wire mesh, and what I have defined 'Metaphysical Ruin', its application on the historical substrate, they are the object of my research aimed at projecting onto the real something that is not there, or that existed and has since disappeared.

The *Basilica of Siponto* is an expression of the Metaphysical Ruin: a sculpture–architecture that suggests the original forms of the monument but is contaminated with the context both visually and spatially, thus delineating itself as a profoundly contemporary artifact.

Int|AR: Your work is read entirely differently when seen in daylight or at night. Does this duality inform the conceptualization of your projects?

ET: Lighting is an integral part of my work in the design phase and, obviously, in its perception. Solid and void are born from light and shadow that impact the wire mesh, sculpting it or merging with it.

OPPOSITE AND ABOVE

Basilica Di Siponto, a permanent installation commissioned by the Ministry
of Cultural Heritage and Activities and Tourism, Manfredonia, Italy, 2016

During the day, atmospheric agents make them dynamic spaces where the boundaries between inside and outside fade away, while at night, artificial lighting enriches surfaces and volumes, characterizing them in suspense and majesty.

> **Int|AR:** In the installation at Le Bon Marché store in Paris, identical forms are displayed but in two different materials: wire mesh and steel. This is the first time that you introduce a second material. What is the significance of this action? Given the properties of each of the materials, the resulting form, though conceptually identical, offer contrasting aspects of the volume. The wire mesh speaks of an ethereal space while the steel reveals the confines of surface. How do you wish your audience to view the two structures?

ET: I am fascinated by most industrial materials. For some time, I wanted to experiment with corrugated sheet metal and found the perfect opportunity with *Aura*, structured on a continuous conceptual dichotomy that I also applied to the material.

Aura is in fact a reflection on the concept of art and architecture, ruin and disintegration, on the passage of time and the transformation of matter through the contrast between classical form and contemporary materials.

The project in wire mesh expresses the spirit of the architectural form, through which absence is evoked, while that in corrugated sheet metal is an organic relic, the empty shell of the architecture. While expressing a dichotomy, the two works are in continuous dialogue with each other: both are pure structural essence and narrate a space-time dimension that does not belong to the present.

> **Int|AR:** In *The Work of Art in the Age of Mechanical Reproduction*, Walter Benjamin states, "...that which withers in the age of mechanical reproduction is the aura of the work of art." You deliberately give the name *Aura* to your project at Le Bon Marché. Can you speak to your intentions in doing this? How do the two domes of different materials reference (or not) Benjamin's idea of 'aura'?

ET: With the two installations of *Aura* I returned to the subject of architectural ruins: one narrates the spiritual dimension, the other the physical.

As fragments of the past and an integral part of the Western imagination, in constant balance between form and anti-form, I believe that the ruins are steeped in the 'Aura' defined by Walter Benjamin, "the unique

Aura, a temporary installation at the Le Bon Marché Rive Gauche, Paris,
France, 2017

appearance of a distance," the magical and supernatural force which emanates from their uniqueness.

Int|AR: Your project *Sacral*, a classical volume of arches, columns and domes, is installed within the industrial setting of the Leonardo da Vinci National Museum of Science and Technology, whose mission is "to narrate the past, interpret the present through new languages, and outline new dimensions through a constant interaction with the surrounding world." It is the only one of your sited installations that contrasts the classical language of architecture with the vocabulary of its host context. What was the impetus for this contrast? And, do you see this strategy as a development from your previous projects working within existing ruins?

ET: *Sacral* was presented in 2016 for the exhibition, *Il Paradiso Inclinato*, at the Ex Dogana of Rome, an industrial space, and was thus born in full contrast with the location. While in Rome, I was fascinated by the potential co-existence of classical forms, materials and industrial locations; in the Science Museum of Milan this co-existence was an opportunity to remind visitors of the historical nature of the building, which over the years was a Benedictine monastery, an Olivetan monastery, then a hospital and a military barracks, until its inauguration as a Museum in 1953. It is a tribute to the space's capacity to adapt to transformations.

Int|AR: You identify as a sculptor. What do you see as the relationship of sculpture to adaptive reuse?

ET: Intervening in the "life" of architecture is simultaneously stimulating and delicate, and requires multidisciplinary approaches for dealing with complex issues in an organic way. Contemporary interventions are enormously interesting as high-profiled proposals related to technology, materials and the concept of respect for the existing, all with the capacity to enhance and validate artistic applications.

ABOVE AND OPPOSITE
Sacral, a temporary installation, *Il Paradiso Inclinato* - Ex Dogana,
Curated by Luca Tomio, Rome, Italy, 2016

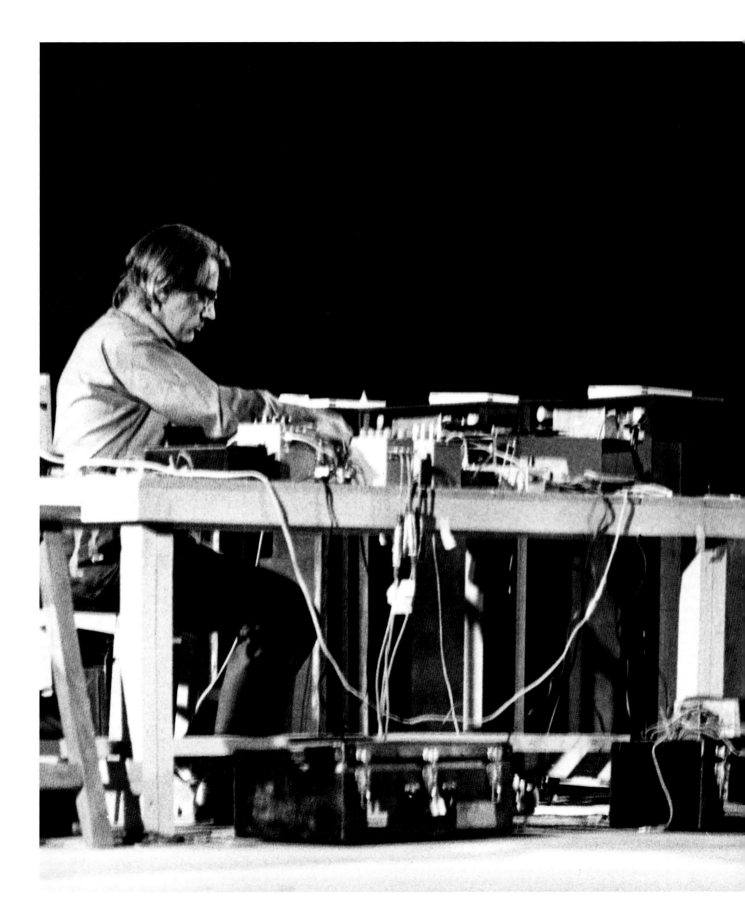

Shiraz Art Festival: David Tudor (L) and John Cage (R) at 1971 festival
Courtesy of Cunningham Dance foundation Archive

THE SONIFEROUS LANDSCAPE

A NEW UNDERSTANDING OF THE SUBLIME

by RANA ABUDAYYEH AND KRAMER WOODARD

Humankind's rapport with nature is an ever-evolving narrative, one of many layers and disjunctive attitudes. Yet underlying this relationship is a reverence for nature that led to the formation of the concept of landscape. In "Eidetic Operations and New Landscapes," James Corner discusses the production of landscape, juxtaposing it to an "unmediated environment." Tracing its conception back to the Old English term Landskip that refers to the picture of land as opposed to its actuality, Corner explains a tendency to contain the natural within frameworks accessible to the human understanding of it.[1] Yet, he clearly acknowledges that such understanding comes on account of considerable detachment from the land itself.[2] Corner's assessment is one of many accounts that depict our ever-changing relationship with nature.

18th century philosopher Edmund Burke defined the term 'sublime' in his treatise, *A Philosophical Enquiry into the Origin of Our Ideas of the Sublime and Beautiful*, "as an artistic effect productive of the strongest emotion the mind is capable of feeling."[3] This concept influenced works of literature, poetry, music and art in the 18th and 19th centuries that probed the immensity of Nature. The paintings of Martin and Turner illustrate such awe for Nature and the landscape. Contemporary approaches towards nature often replace this reverence with logic, the logic of understanding its systems and further dominating it with the multitude of manmade mechanisms.[4] A quick survey of one's surroundings reveals overexposed settings conditioned and processed through a myriad of apparatuses and digital streams. Machines are as common place to the wilderness as the blade of grass. Contrails and pavement streak the air and land while the wakes of ships part the waves of the oceans and lakes. We accept this intrusion and in many ways have come to believe it is proof that we

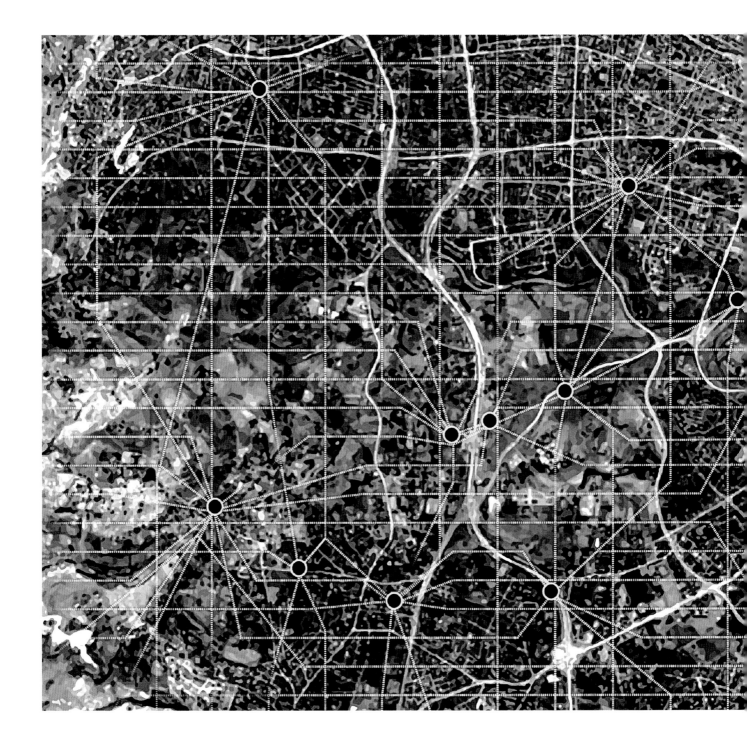

are in charge of nature and can, through our technology, control it. Therein lies a predicament in trying to reconcile the concept of the sublime with the reality of man's heavy-handed manipulation of nature. But what of the innate gravitation towards the natural sublime? Do we fully acknowledge that the raw unadulterated natural ceases to exist and accept its replacement with a hybrid sublime, a fabricated one?

Kant defined the sublime in juxtaposition to the beautiful, a catalyst to mental agitation as opposed to restful contemplation.[5] This agitation which triggers a sense of pleasure, hinges on suspending the comprehension of the object of the sublime and accepting a measure of ambiguity in our assessment of context. While the tendency for establishing the sublime has often relied on "manipulation of scale, monumentality, and light"[6] the optic dependency of our current digital culture necessitates a broader employment of sensory

Mapping Soundscapes, by the authors

A map of the southwestern quadrant of Amman, Jordan, locating the mosques in that area. The location of the mosques (marked by a yellow circle) displaces an imposed grid

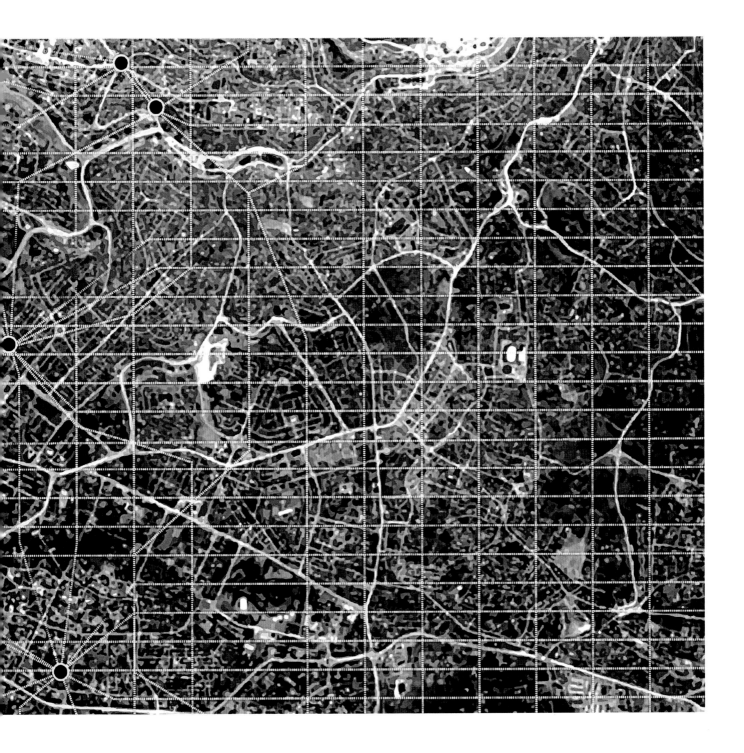

stimuli. This is echoed in Corner's advocacy for imaging the landscape through practices that do not prioritize a dependency on visual and formal tendencies, rather, encompass a mental conception that is equally acoustic and tactile.[7]

A precedent for such multi-sensory imaging can be found in the sublime landscape paintings of the 19th century. These painting are both extraordinarily and equally frightening depictions of the power of nature.

In Turner's *The Slave Ship*, originally titled *Slavers Throwing Overboard the Dead and Dying—Typhoon Coming On*, the direness of the scene is depicted through nature's turbulence and wrath. The inflamed sea churning in opposition to our human acts appeals to our conscience through sound as much as image. While these sounds are silenced by the medium of paint and the techniques of painting, they define—by the virtue of their visual depiction—a deafening loudness.

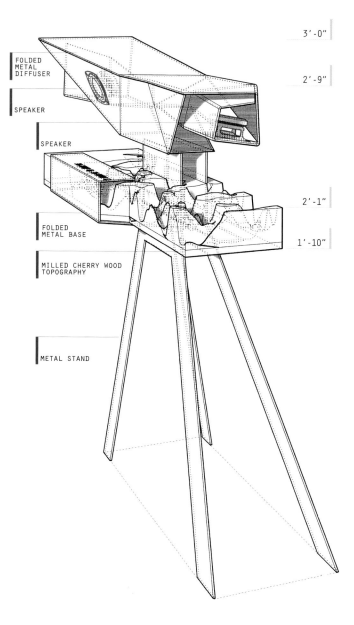

FOLDED
METAL
DIFFUSER

SPEAKER

SPEAKER

FOLDED
METAL BASE

MILLED CHERRY WOOD
TOPOGRAPHY

METAL STAND

3'-0"

2'-9"

2'-1"

1'-10"

techniques, however, could be employed in the service of poignant narratives that integrate critical aesthetics with other sensory experiences of everyday life such as sound. In the example of Turner, establishing acoustic practices as narration mediums would allow one to hear his interventions. As a result, the sublime shifts from absolute ambiguity (as per its Kantian definition) to ambiguous reoccurrences that challenge the prevalent optical dependencies of the latter. Here, we as subjects accept its deviation from its previous depictions of grandeur to new transitory states of suspension of reason, in between understandings, at once, unsettled and anchored through the soniferous provocations of context.

The Spatial Agency of Sound

In describing his piece *Imaginary Landscapes No.4*, composer John Cage writes, "The sounds enter the time-space centered within themselves, unimpeded by the service to any abstraction, their 360 degrees of circumference free for an infinite play of interpenetration. Value judgments are not in the nature of this work as regards either composition, performance, or listening. The idea of relation being absent, anything may happen. A mistake is beside the point, for once anything happens it authentically is."[8]

Linked to a different understanding of time and place, Cage's *Imaginary Landscapes No.4* challenged through its framework the temporality and relevance of sound. Performed by twenty-four players and a conductor using twelve radios to output sounds, the piece morphed depending on the time and place of its execution, transcending the common tropes of permanence and reproduction that are often linked to the making of place.

The synthesis of space and place has often relied primarily on visual stimuli. Provocations associated with spatial constructs identify primarily with appearances. Designers manipulate the appearances of things, their representations, putting forth a calculated image of what is to be conveyed. Sound on the other hand, postures an authenticity that resists as Cage puts it "abstraction." As such, sound is one of the more bona fide gauges of spatial identity. Furthermore, soniferous parameters transcend the limitations of anchoring to contextual parameters; they establish when disseminated a complete setting capable of adaptation and reanimation by virtue of their variability between activity and dormancy.

Understanding the faculty of sound in design is contingent on understanding the act of hearing itself. Jonathan Sterne describes hearing saying, "it is human nature and human history, deeply personal and irreducibly intersubjective, environmentally grounded and stretched towards transcendence."[9] The human narrative is one that is well rooted within an auditory tradition. Yet, the agency of the auditory registry lies in

Turner's soniferous interventions are not audible, yet, they exist; one can hear the sounds of the crashing waves and the cries of the dying. They further persist in their telling—through an emphasis on nature—of a poignant narrative that is as pertinent now as it was then.

Turner's work is exemplary of the sublime in its day. And yet in its intense evocation of nature lies the potential of new understandings and translations of the sublime today. In recent history, we have seen the rise of many industries such as the blockbuster movie, mega concert attractions, widescreen cinematic sound, and virtual and augmented reality which exploit through newfound techniques our fascination with the sublime. Rendering the richness of the sublime to fixes, fads, and highs, such approaches present experiences void of any critical narrative and reflection on nature. These same

A digital drawing showing the components of one of the soniferous vessels.

A Full-Scale Study Model of a Typical Vessel, by the authors

Displayed in the fabrication lab, the vessel was the first physical iteration of
the project unit. Blue tooth wireless speaker we used to test the folded steel
plate sound diffusers, and calibrate the milled wood landscape to achieve the
desired emission patterns

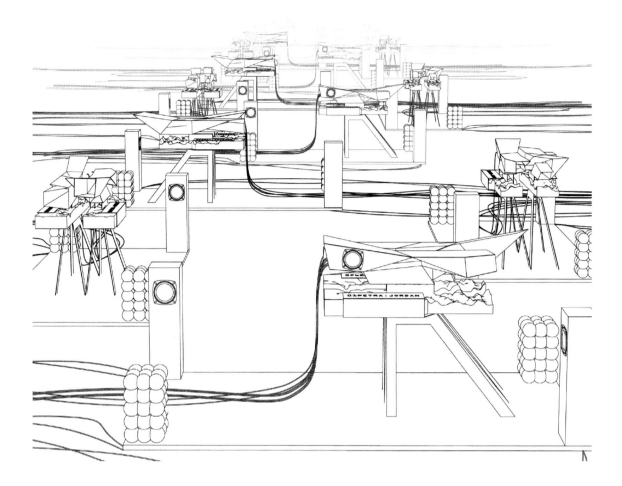

its recursive mutations and improvisations; the variation carried by each alteration is telling of hidden narratives and registers that reveal climactic nuances often inaccessible to other narration mediums. This metabolism is unique to sound and engenders renewable readings of space, time, and place. According to Sterne, "to understand the faculty of audition is, then, simultaneously to understand its possibilities and its limits, its status as embedded in real social relations, and its power as a figurative and imaginative metaphor for other registers of human action."[10]

Despite sound's integral role in the human narrative, its expressions remain rather limited when compared to visuality, especially in spatial design, which has often invested in strategies to dampen or enhance sounds in service of programmatic needs. However, can the soniferous be employed to cater to narratives and provocations in the same manner as the visual often is? Compelling as it may be to position one mode of narration medium against the other, the fact remains that only through the alliance of various modalities are narrative environments evoked. A soniferous landscape is therefore not exclusive to sound, rather, they bargain on the amalgamation of various sensory modalities.

Despite these interwoven dependencies, they establish their climatic sublimation through an intentional favoring of the auditory, presenting the visual as the constant and sound as the variable.

Narratives of the New Sublime

Over the course of a mere couple of hundred years of human activities, acoustic landscapes have changed dramatically from a higher to lower based frequency;[11] this is largely the result of machine technologies and is particularly true in urban areas. *The Soniferous Landscape* is a series of miniaturized artificial terrains modeled after real sites and activated by sound. This project sets out to explore the landscape of sound and its effects on our perception of space. The installation comprises vessels arrayed in space. Each vessel is composed of folded sheet steel, cherry wood, and two speakers mounted on the folded metal sound diffuser. The sound emitted bounces off a milled cherry wood topography. The topographic surface variations contribute to an audible change in the pitch and volume, while the visual impact of the milled ridges, peaks and valleys invoke the reading of a shift in sound. Enhanced by the dysmorphic topographies of the machined wood, audio

The Soniferous Landscape, Connective Structure, by the authors
A digital drawing showing the connective systems of wires and speakers woven throughout the installation's vessels

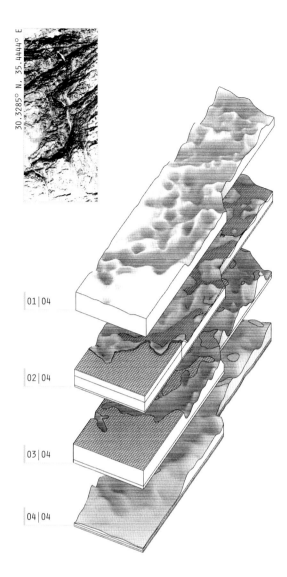

30.3285° N, 35.4444° E

01|04

02|04

03|04

04|04

fabric of place. Despite the minarets' multitude and heavy physical presence, what one recalls is not necessarily their appearance, rather, it is the soniferous scape they cyclically define. At times, the sound of the call for prayer carries through the sharpness of the atmosphere and at others, it is dampened by the heavy humidity in the air. It informs time, weather, and the direction of prevailing winds. It ushers people into choreographed events and interactions; streams of home lights flicker during the first early dawn minutes in response, while stamping of feet follow. Traditionally, the call for prayer was recited by a person (the muezzin) atop the minarets facing the Kiblah (the direction to which Muslims turn to prayer). As such, the call had limited projection; however, in modern times, recordings get emitted from speakers mounted on top of the minarets. The slightly off-synced sound of the recorded calls going out resonates off the urban scape of the city. The numerous multiplications of the collective sounds echoing off various structures possess a sublime effect.

This man-made occurrence, a staple of a Middle Eastern setting, is neither unpleasant nor beautiful per se, and its effects are rather visceral. Nonetheless, it does not follow the conventional stream of the sublime as it challenges common associations with Nature. Here, the structured references to or associations with[14] is not between man and nature, rather man and the man-made. The sound penetrates the intimate interiority of place with or without invitation, and engulf the dweller, making him/her part of a collective presence. To appraise or analyze this event is rather impossible as it resists the common assessment of beauty and/ or distastefulness. A soniferous landscape as such finds definition in a new understanding of the sublime. Building on this is a mapping of the location of a number of mosques in the southwestern quadrant of the city of Amman. The locations of the mosques (marked by a yellow circle) displaces an imposed grid. The magnitude of this alteration is based on the size of the mosque and the density of the neighborhood it serves, projecting by its visual registers the interference cause by the sound of the dawn prayer call. The resulting grid functions as the locator for the sound vessels of the installation, using the distorted areas of the grid to place the vessels.

The Landscape and its Exhibition

In our contemporary era of digital imagery, the landscape has contended with exponential miniaturizing and flattening imposed by virtual media. The ubiquity of such affects carried significant implications on our attitude towards context and issued in a disassociation (or in the least a different association) with place. Miniaturizing the landscape through this installation reflects on this equivocal relationship engendered by advanced technology and references the sublime's association

drivers associated with motion sensors, displace sound; delocalizing its source and projected destinations. Using the installation as both an experiment and demonstration of a soniferous sublime, the project examines the role and potential inherent in acoustic stimuli as narration mediums of the landscape. Here, the interior volume is the site where this acoustically driven account occurs, shifting the common role of architecture in the subliminal experience. Traditionally, interior space functioned as the shelter in which one sought protection from natural forces,[12] that protection provided by architecture enabled the experience of the sublime. Through this installation, such roles reverse. Interior space becomes the realm where the soniferous is disseminated, seeking as such new plateaus and readings of the sublime attuned to places that carry a unique sonic footprint.[13]

This particular series of miniature terrains is derived from a Middle Eastern setting where minarets are a common occurrence and play an integral role in the

Serial Terrains, by the authors

Serial digital models depicting the terrain of Petra [0.3285° N, 35.4444° E]. While the terrains developed in this series began with a Google Earth image

of Petra, Jordan, the image underwent a series digital tooling acts. Each recursive alteration distances the landscape from the source image, resulting in a series of four alias landscapes

65

with nature. What does it mean to be sitting in your living room and scan the entirety of the globe, from its remote wilderness to its most populated metropolis? What does it mean to visit every city, and wander every street by the drag of the cursor of your computer? Google Earth imaging is only one example of the shift in our relationship to context that gave rise to many parallel natures of sorts. Vast landscapes distilled to frozen frames and reanimated through streams of data, delivered via a compressed binary code to the comfort of your interior abode. Peter Eisenman alluded to this new reality saying, "The electronic paradigm directs a challenge to architecture because it defines reality in terms of media and simulation, it values appearance over existence, what can be seen over what is."[15] It is precisely this focus on manufactured appearances that *The Soniferous Landscape* seeks to challenge, retelling the narratives of place by values of sounds and haptic interactions.

While the terrains developed in this series began with a Google Earth image of the mountainous terrain of Petra, Jordan, the image underwent a series of digital tooling acts. Each of the vessel was placed on a slightly different topography of Petra, enabling subtle variations in the emitted sounds. Each recursive alteration distances the landscape from the source image, resulting in a series of four alias landscapes. Milled out of cherry wood, a species that is foreign to the region, these aliases assume further artificiality. Suspended in-between the narrative and the manifest, they question the reliability of reading the environment via virtual instrumentalities and pose a paradoxical claim; even though modern means enabled a scientific understanding of the environment, these readings are by no means infallible. It is only through this fallibility that our sense of the natural persists, and finds the space for the imaginative, the ambiguous...the sublime.

Soniferous Ecologies

The Soniferous Landscape makes the case for our ever-present relationship with nature while acknowledging a change in our attitude towards it. Retelling a new version of an old story, standing at 36" high, the installation's vessels decontextualize the terrain, and displace the soundscape, shifting the scalar prominence from nature to the occupant, from the expanse to the interior volume. Unfettered by the taxonomy of time and space, the installation narrates a new environment of fragments and incompatible components. It tells the stories of distant lands using foreign tongues and familiar places. It appeals to our senses and sensibilities while asking us to momentarily suspend our logic.

While the need for the sublime has occupied the human imaginative for centuries and presented powerful means of narration and influence, a new technological era laden with an abundance of visual stimuli threatens its annulment. A new understanding of the

sublime offers sound as the narrative driver, an alternate to the overload of visual accounts that define our current technologically driven environments. It builds on oral histories and traditions, and thus allows for a measure of acoustic distortion to take place. It is established via altering the artificial landscape, be it the milled topographic reproduction of the installation or the arrangement of the urban setting; this distortion yields the subliminal experience. Rather than being the object of the sublime, the landscape becomes its catalyst, facilitating by this change of roles a new assessment of the object and objective of the sublime narrative.

ENDNOTES:

1 Corner, J. *Recovering landscape: Essays in contemporary landscape architecture* (New York: Princeton Architectural Press, 2006) 153.

2 Ibid, p. 155

3 https://www.tate.org.uk/art/art-terms/s/sublime, accessed 10 March 2019.

4 Kate Nesbitt. "The Sublime and Modern Architecture: Unmasking (An Aesthetic Of) Abstraction." *New Literary History* 26, no. 1 (1995): 98. http://www.jstor.org/stable/20057270

5 Immanuel Kant and Werner S. Pluhar. *Critique of Judgment* (Indianapolis, Ind: Hackett, 2010), 101.

6 Kate Nesbitt. "The Sublime and Modern Architecture: Unmasking (An Aesthetic Of) Abstraction." *New Literary History* 26, no. 1 (1995): 101. http://www.jstor.org/stable/20057270

7 Corner, J. *Recovering landscape: Essays in contemporary landscape architecture* (New York: Princeton Architectural Press, 2006) 153.

8 John Cage, *Silence: Lectures and Writing* (Middletown: Wesleyan University Press, 1973) 59.

9 Matt Sakakeeny, *Keywords in Sound* (Durham: Duke University Press, 2015), 65, ProQuest Ebook Central.

10 Ibid.

11 Bryan C. Pijanowski et al., "Soundscape Ecology: The Science of Sound in the Landscape," *BioScience* Volume 61, Issue 3 (1 March 2011): 209, https://doi.org/10.1525/bio.2011.61.3.6

12 Kate Nesbitt. *Theorizing a New Agenda for Architecture: An Anthology of Architectural Theory* 1965-1995 (New York: Princeton Architectural Press, 2008), 49.

13 Bryan C. Pijanowski et al., "Soundscape Ecology: The Science of Sound in the Landscape," *BioScience* Volume 61, Issue 3 (1 March 2011): 203, https://doi.org/10.1525/bio.2011.61.3.6

14 Kate Nesbitt. "The Sublime and Modern Architecture: Unmasking (An Aesthetic Of) Abstraction." *New Literary History* 26, no. 1 (1995): 97. http://www.jstor.org/stable/20057270

15 Peter Eisenman. "Visions' Unfolding: Architecture in the Age of Electronic Media," *Domus*, 734 (Jan 1992), 21.

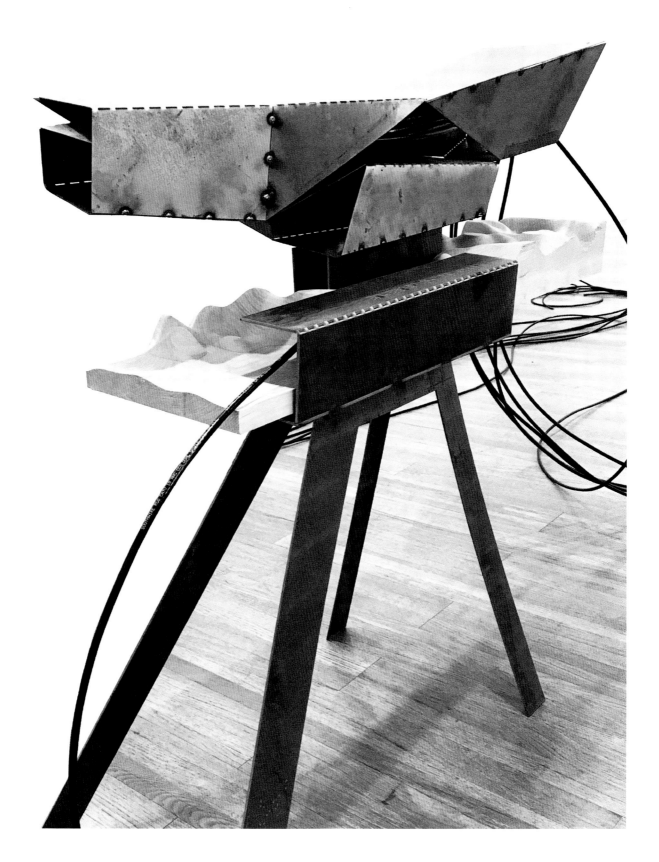

A Soniferous Vessel, by the authors

A photo of the final vessel design using variation # 04 of site 0.3285° N, 35.4444° E. The vessel is 36" high, composed of milled cherry wood, folded steel plate sound diffusers and equipped with two speakers

BETWEEN THE SACRED AND THE MUNDANE

by ALOK BHASIN AND PUJA ANAND

Benaras is older than history, older than tradition, older even than legend and looks twice as old as all of them put together.

—Mark Twain[1]

Located in the Gangetic plains of India, and sited on the banks of River Ganga, Varanasi (also known as Benaras colloquially and mentioned as Kashi in the ancient scriptures and texts) is one of the oldest living cities of the world. Revered by the adherents of the Dharmic religions (Hinduism, Buddhism and Jainism) this city holds a sacred place in the collective minds of the people of these faiths and is considered the spiritual capital of India. For ages, Varanasi has been a center of learning for philosophy, spirituality, mysticism, Yoga, Tantra and other branches of traditional Indian learning.

Since antiquity, Varanasi has both intrigued and attracted people in equal measures and continues to do so. Religious leaders, wandering ascetics and philosophers have been drawn to this city and its many Ghats (Bathing steps), while poets, writers, artists and photographers flock to this place, seeking solace or to gain inspiration. Not to be left behind are the tourists and the students of culture and history, and in the midst of this influx of outsiders, live the actual inhabitants of the city who continue with their daily lives on these Ghats, praying, bathing, washing, cooking and also carrying on commerce as seen in the various shops, food and tea stalls. Amid this business of living also exists the business of dying.

The tangible as well as intangible coexist in Varanasi, in the form of its rich and vibrant culture, and especially embodied in the cultural landscapes of the Ghats of the river Ganga. Stretching across a 2.5 mile long riverbank of Varanasi, are situated 84 Ghats (Bathing steps). These Ghats are man-made structures that have sprung up through the ages, and have continued to evolve and react to the changing needs of the users of these spaces. These Ghats of the riverfront constitute the tangible heritage, including fortresses, palaces, monastic buildings, and guest houses for the travelers, places of learning, along with the numerous temples that literally dot the landscape. The Intangible heritage is reflected in the socioreligious customs and rites of passage, and also the various artists, craftsmen, yoga practitioners practicing their craft. Here the traditional way of life continues to exist in spite of the modernity that has crept in and is engulfing the lifestyle of the city. Thus, the connections between the river with the religious and cultural ethos of the city and the profound impact of these on the economic and social life of the city is a unique amalgamation of the tangible and the intangible.[2]

The Ghat is both a poetic concept and a real, physical place that can be traversed and observed, superimposing

Sadhus with holy ash smeared faces, siting with devotees; tea-seller.

the imagined over the actual, and for the visitor the result
is an immersive experience; an experience that can be
visceral yet holistic, full of impressions that affect all the
five senses. The Ghats are thus an embodiment of the
public space, assuming the form of a public
commons, and at the same time, act as a private space
where the visitor/devotee engages in performing their
ablutions and rituals, ensconced in their own space
bubble, immune to the gaze of the onlooker.

The Sacred Aspects

Considered the abode of Lord Shiva, Varanasi has
existed from time immemorial. Varanasi (or Kashi as
it is known in ancient Hindu texts) is older than traditions and presents a unique combination of physical,
metaphysical and supernatural elements. As per Hindu
beliefs, one who dies in Varanasi would attain salvation
and freedom from the cycle of birth and re-birth.
The Ganga Ghats are perhaps the holiest spots of

People bathing and washing clothes in the holy water

Varanasi, and bring the mundane world in contact with the Divine. The River Ganga (Ganges) in Varanasi is believed to have the power to wash away the sins of mortals and the Ghats are visited by thousands of pilgrims every day to take a dip in the holy river and to perform rituals and ceremonies. The Sacredness is affirmed daily at the Ghats through rituals and the veneration of river goddess.

The Ghats act as repositories for cultural memories, stories and myths, and at the same time are settings for continuation of ancient practices and rituals that are still an important aspect of the religious life for most Hindus. Coming down the steps through the narrow streets and alleys, one comes up to the openness of the Ghats; thus in a way, the experiences of the visitor is of a haptic and multisensory type. This symbolizes the journey from the darkness to enlightenment and from the mundane towards the holy. Public and private life are interspersed cheerfully, as the residents go about their daily life in the midst of the intrusive tourism. Thus commercial, recreational and social activities as well as the religious ones occur in a hodgepodge that is orderly in its own chaotic way. For an observer new to this city, the apparent chaos is disconcerting, but there exists a method in this very madness, and this has what has sustained the Ghats for so long and has contributed to the exalted place of Varanasi. A visit to the Ghats in the early hours of the morning presents a sight of people offering their morning prayers, paying their obsequies to the rising sun; the evening brings a delightful and awe-inspiring spectacle of the Ganga Aarti.

Just like the glimpses of daily life that one encounters at these Ghats, one sees Death too and nowhere is the business of dying more manifest than at the two main Cremation Ghats of Varanasi: Harishchandra Ghat and Manikarnika Ghat, reputed to be the cremation grounds where there is a funeral pyre burning always. As per Hindu beliefs, cremation at these Ghats ensures Moksha (salvation) for the departed soul. Thus, Hindus from distant places bring the dead bodies of their relatives to these Ghats for cremation.

The sights and the smells of burning bodies on smoking pyres, the almost endless funeral processions accompanied by throngs of mourners chanting Ram Nam Satya Hai (The Name of God is the eternal Truth), all of these serve as a reminder to the mortals that Death is the final Truth, an inalienable part of the cycle of life.

Festivals and Fairs

It is said that every day is a festival in Benares and this is seen in the various festivals and fairs that happen on the Ghats of Varanasi, based on the waxing and waning of the moon, prescribed by the ancient Hindu calendar. Due to its exalted religious and cultural significance, Varanasi plays host to a plethora of festivals and holy observances all through the year. Apart from the regular festivals and holy observances that are common throughout the Hindu world like Deepawali, Holi, etc, there are important festivals dedicated to a particular deity or the other nearly every month.

The festival of Dev Deepavali is held on the full moon day in the month of Kartik (also known as Kartik Purnima, which is a sacred day for Hindus, Sikhs and Jains), when the Gods are believed to descend to the earth from the heavens. This festival is observed with great fanfare and feasts. In the evening, pilgrims and local residents decorate the entire riverbank with tiny earthen lamps ('Diya'). These lamps are lit as a mark of welcome to the Gods as they descend on earth.

Apart from these festivals, many Melas (Fairs) are also held at Varanasi. Ganga Mahotsav is a 4-day festival organized by the Uttar Pradesh Tourism department to showcase the rich cultural heritage of Varanasi, with/ performers coming to perform at the celebrations held at Dashashwamedh Ghat.

These festivals and fairs are celebrated with traditional fervor but also show signs of encroaching modernity. Performers and mendicants dressed up as Gods try to make a living out of the piety of the pilgrims, bringing the overlaps of the sordidness of the commercial on the religious aspects.

The Mundane

Notwithstanding the especial place of Varanasi in the Sacred landscape of Hindu thought and philosophy, the city is still a living place, host to a teeming population going about the business of living. Thus, apart from the religiousness of the Ghats of Varanasi, signs of daily life are omnipresent here. One can see boat-builders repairing and building boats; boatmen accosting passersby and visitors, promising rides along and across the river at a good price; fishermen with their catch, or sitting mending their nets; barbers looking for custom; masseurs specializing in traditional massage to help heal the body cramps that the bathers get after a dip in the river; clothes drying on balustrade railings, and sometimes even on the steps of the Ghats. And then there are the tea-stalls selling tea and snacks, kiosks selling tobacco, cigarettes and betel leaves, ambulant hawkers selling more tea and light snacks. In the midst of these, one can also find sellers hawking religious paraphernalia and touristy trinkets and souvenirs. The walls of the Ghats are replete with murals of gods and goddesses, signs advertising tuitions for learning Hindi and Sanskrit, advertisements for internet cafes, pizzerias, cafes and restaurants catering to the western palates.

Throw in impressive palaces, temples, dilapidated houses, guest homes, hospices for the dying, crumbling mansions once owned by the rich and the famous of India, the royalty and the philanthropists, monastic houses for mendicants, even an observatory.
Add to this mix, children playing cricket, girls playing with dolls, sacred cows roaming around, and the not-so-sacred dogs sleeping or running around, amid the cacophony of the river ducks and geese, all make for a moving palimpsest of life, both divine and otherwise.

Caught betwixt the Sacred and the Mundane

The concept of a Teertha (ford) is brought to life in the Ghats, and they act as thresholds for the Sacredness, and at the same time, also play host to a rich social life of the Benarsis (as residents of Varanasi are called) and the many tourists who visit here. In this way, the liminal nature of the Ghats embody both the Sacred and the Mundane. While the Sacred is seen in and around the Ghats through the rites and rituals of the faithful, it is in exactly these places that everyday life is inexorably woven in. While the linear spatiality of the Ghats reaching down to the liminal spaces where the devotees meet the river, there are spaces and volumes carved out within the Ghats themselves. These spaces house Gods (in the form of lingas and statues) or humans (of both the sacred and the mundane type in the form of Sadhus, yoga practitioners and barbers and petty stall-holders selling the paraphernalia of both the sacred and the mundane).

As the boatman promises crossings of the river for a price, so does the priest who assures of a crossover or fording across the threshold between the mundane world towards the one of godliness and salvation. This cheek-by-jowl coexistence of avarice and greed and the quest for things spiritual as well as temporal brings to light the duality of life at the Ghats.

Conclusion

The tangible heritage of Varanasi's history is sometimes manifested in the form of its buildings, especially along the Ghats. However, behind the tangible lie the unseen and intangible aspects that have deep symbolism and sacred importance for the people who dwell here as well as those who visit this place. In fact, it is the intangible aspects like skills, stories, rituals and cultural practices that form the basic foundation for the actual cultural heritage that is visible. This intangible cultural heritage has also continued to evolve to reflect the influences and interactions of Varanasi's traditional culture vis-à-vis modern life.

The Ghats are a backdrop for performances and narratives, where some of the performances are routine and humdrum, but some are dramatic in nature. Some are sacred, and some are mundane, and some are both as the sacred and mundane aspects overlap. The local residents, the tourists, the ascetics, the students of culture and history, are all drawn towards these Ghats, for they offer a diorama of sorts, encompassing ancient scriptures, mythologies, cultural practices. From christenings and hair-shoring rituals of newborns to cremations of the dead, the Ghats of Ganga are a static yet continuously evolving display of all that passes in a person's life journey. The people who have used these spaces have constructed their own meanings and responses to the contexts and sub-contexts. The deep cohesions between space and the users, affected by culture and customs and social needs is visible in these Ghats and which have adapted themselves to newer modern contexts.

The Ghats of Varanasi are hard to define: at once repulsive and sensual, frightening as well as enticing, irrational and yet spiritually enlightening. At the heart of this ambiguity lies the particular charm of the riverfront spaces, and combined with the religious and secular aspects of life along the Ghats, this liminality between the cultural and spatial, and the absence of this liminality at the same time, is what constitutes the living heritage of this place, and can be seen and appreciated.[3]

The sheer diversity of the visitors to the Ghats, both Indian and foreigners, the backdrop of the secular and religious architecture, the juxtaposition of the ritual, the commercial and the recreational aspects; the inseparable ideas of the Public and the Private space; the concept of Life and Death, spirituality and temporality; all make the Ghats a theatre of life, with culture being performed, and the tourists and visitors are unwitting participants and audience as well as actors on this stage, ultimately becoming a part of the cultural landscape. This assumes the form of Living Heritage, something that continues to evolve and still is rooted in tradition. The tourist finds curiosities and exotic images, and the seeker of things spiritual finds his inner peace here.

Steeped in history, and carrying with them the many stories and tales about myths, historical events, religious practices, cultural mores, and rituals, it is these riverside Ghats that act as a permanent exhibit, an exhibit that is a witness to the evolution of collective thought of India, its peoples and its cultures. It is here that the past and the present can be seen together, as a veritable feast for the eyes as well as the mind. As part of the urban fabric of this ancient city, it is well-nigh impossible to separate the sacred from the mundane, and can be seen as parts of a dynamic with many layers, sharing a spatial as well as a temporal narrative.

ENDNOTES:

1 Mark Twain, *Following the Equator: A Journey around the World,* (Hartford, 1897), 36.

2 Richard Lannoy, *Benares Seen from Within,* (London, John Martin, 1999), 10.

3 Richard King, *Orientalism and Religion: Postcolonial Theory, India and 'The Mystic East',* (London: Taylor & Francis e-Library, 2001), 82-95.

CULTURAL AMBASSADORS

ALLOPATRIC ADAPTIVE REUSE AND SECONDARY NARRATIVES

by HONGJIANG WANG

The original narrative of Huizhou folk dwellings

Huizhou merchants dominated the Chinese business community for nearly 500 years during the Ming (1368–1644) and Qing (1644–1911) Dynasties, and these merchants, who traveled far from their hometowns, accumulated enormous wealth by selling salt, tea, rice and other commodities. Many successful Huizhou merchants returned to their hometowns located in today's Huangshan City and Jixi County in Anhui Province, and Wuyuan in Jiangxi Province, where they built many exquisite dwellings and ancestral halls. Now, few descendants, whose forefathers lived in the 7,000 folk houses of more than 100 ancient villages in Huizhou district, are still willing to live in these dim ancestral houses. In addition to some outstanding dwellings that were protected and repaired by local governments at various levels, some scattered old houses that were not on the protection list in the early years were purchased by outsiders. These neglected houses have benefitted from relocation and adaptive reuse. In the era of globalization, some excellent dwellings rebuilt in other places have become cultural ambassadors of spatial narratives through their distinctive architectural and symbolic features.

Architectural narrative endows a place with identifiability and memorability through stories, establishing a connection between people and space. The first narration of Huizhou folk dwellings, which are regarded as the physical shelter and spiritual home of Huizhou merchants, is based on a unique residential culture. In the humid monsoon climate and beautiful hilly environment, the site selection and spatial layout, guided by the Feng Shui theory of Zhouyi, embody the unity of man and nature in traditional Chinese philosophy and its

A Huizhou settlement in the Xixinan town of the Anhui province in China

Wood-carving panels under windows are a feature of Huizhou dwellings

respect for nature. The introverted living philosophy and the spiritual beliefs of Huizhou merchants, also known as Confucian traders, were conveyed through the home's protective inward spatial order, as well as the application of wood, brick and stone carving crafts as symbolic narrative elements. These decorative crafts, which were carved on the beams, pillars, doors, windows, entrance walls, etc. mostly describe animal and plant patterns that symbolize auspiciousness and good luck. Character images from Chinese folklore and literary tales conveyed the owner's desire for a better life by using rhetorical devices such as metaphor, metonymy and synecdoche. They employ a basic narrative method similar to that of murals and sculpture in Western churches. Generally speaking, the original space narrators of Huizhou housing were not professional architects, but home owners and folk craftsmen. They iteratively developed the architectural style based on local customs and accumulated experience and gradually formed the cultural semantics of Huizhou housing as a unique narrative.

The secondary narrative in relocated sites

With the development of economic globalization and the rapid dissemination of information, this architecture has gradually become a symbol of politics, capital, and culture, separated from the existing place spirit and life experience. After the original residential space was translocated to public cultural places, such as museums, new stories were implanted from its reconstruction. In the process of demolition, transportation, restoration and adaptive reuse, a secondary narrative is generated, one which merges the migrated Huizhou housing with the local culture. Yin Yu Tang, which opened in the Peabody Essex Museum, Salem, MA in 2003, is one such example. The story began with American Nancy Berliner's chance encounter with the Ancient House of the Huang Family, located in Xiuning County, Anhui Province. Nancy, who loved Chinese culture, met the Huang family in 1996 as they were preparing to sell their ancestral house. They immediately made a deal. The demolition of the house the following year took

Yin Yu Tang, Salem, MA

four months and 2,735 wooden components, 972 stone pieces, together with the living goods placed in the house, and even the paving stones at the entrance, were removed. In the Spring Festival of 1998, nearly forty containers carrying these articles crossed the Pacific Ocean. This normal ancient dwelling was reborn on the other side of the Pacific Ocean through a careful reconstruction in 2003 and became a sensational story in the Sino-American folk cultural exchanges of that year. Years later, Qiuhua Huang, the 36th generation descendant of the Huang family, stood in the former ancestral house in Salem, a small town near Boston, USA, listening to Yo-Yo Ma's cello performance in the courtyard, and could not help but burst into tears. This sense of sorrow and joy was triggered by the architectural cultural genes that carried the nostalgic memory of the family. As the members of the original family were involved in the migration and reconstruction of the old dwelling, and contributed a large number of precious documents such as daily necessities, genealogy and old photos, the story of the reconstruction was complete and vivid.[1] Because of its relocation and reconstruction, both the original and the secondary narratives of this legendary dwelling are completely represented on the PEM's official website, yinyutang.pem.org.

On the campus of Shanghai Institute of Visual Arts (SIVA), three ancient Huizhou dwellings with a total area of 2,450 square meters are another case of adaptive reuse. Unlike the Yin Yu Tang Museum in the United States, which preserves the original narrative as much as possible, the reconstruction of Huizhou dwellings at SIVA focuses on dynamic reuse rather than static spatial display, providing a large number of secondary narratives. The three ancient dwellings were all built in the late Qing Dynasty, with a history of nearly 200 years. Two of them were purchased by a private collector in 2005 and transferred to SIVA in 2012. After their reconstruction in Shanghai from 2013 to 2014, the former Lin Family House was transformed into the Double-snug Tea House, the characteristic gathering space of SIVA's teaching staff, and the Ancient House of the Xu Family an inclusive multi-functional academic research center. The Zhuangyuan House, which was newly purchased from Leping county, Jiangxi in 2014, has been transformed into a teaching building of the School of Cultural Relics Restoration of SIVA. During the three-year process, a team of SIVA leaders and professional architects reconstructed the surrounding environment, spatial form and interior furnishings of the building. A comprehensive design of architecture, landscape and interior has successfully transformed the ancient folk houses from private residence to public space, completely reshaping the spirit of the place. The user acquires a brand-new spatial cognitive experience based on newly inserted functions. "It is the value orientation and goal of architectural narrative to investigate and evaluate the social and cultural significance of spatial construction by considering the built environment and the life it carries as a whole."[2]

The move of the Lin and Xu Family dwellings from

The Huizhou-style community relocated to the Shanghai Institute of Visual Arts

A Huizhou house with a new use as SIVA's Double–snug Tea House

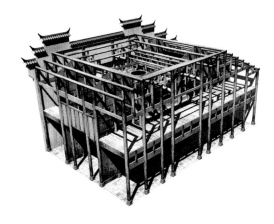

exterior wall, independent of the original wood-frame system, which greatly reduced the pressure on the aged wooden frame. In addition, the old and new structures were horizontally connected by pre-embedded steel bars. On the interior, new brick floor tiles made in the ancient method replaced the old tiles broken during the dismantlement. Missing wooden components were replaced according to the original building, using a restoration technology for traditional residences.

When the Huizhou ancient dwellings were rebuilt at SIVA, the houses, according to the original characteristics, maintained the north entrance in layout, the iconic Ma Tau Wall and the black-white tone in appearance. Due to changes mandated by both the new site and the new functions, however, the houses differed from the originals in both the exterior and interior. New narrative elements have been implanted. For example, the lotus pond and the curved bridge in the courtyard, together with transplanted trees, were added to the site, constituting a garden landscape that echoed the local Jiangnan culture in Shanghai. In order to enrich the architectural form and the outdoor space experience, the original simple south facades of the Lin and Xu Family dwellings were amended with wooden wind and rain corridors, as well as larger, richly detailed doors and windows. Skylights were introduced to bring more natural light to the second floor. A glass roof was added to the atrium space to provide a sheltered outdoor patio. The original low beams were increased by 300mm to improve the usability of the academic center on the second floor. The old narrow and steep stairs were widened. Fire protection requirements such as smoke alarm, sprinkler systems, VRV central air conditioners were introduced in inconspicuous locations.

Alumni of the School of Design at SIVA run the Double-snug Tea House. The refreshing tea as well as the gentle background music of the Chinese zither enrich the details of the secondary narrative and spatial cognition of Chinese traditional culture through taste, smell and hearing. These preserved classical spaces with their Chinese traditional cultural temperament offer the faculty and students stories that have traveled through hundreds of years of history. There is a coexistence of past and present lives in what has become the spiritual home of SIVA.

A similar case of adaptive reuse can be found at Singapore University of Technology and Design (SUTD) where four Zhejiang ancient architectural structures were donated in 2015 by Jackie Chan, the famous Chinese kung fu superstar. They have been carefully reconstructed by the university and serve as an immersive space for displaying ancient Chinese architectural culture as well as for hosting various performances. The two dwellings by a lake, a stage and a pavilion on the lawn are extremely popular on campus and have become the landmarks of SUTD.

Anhui to Shanghai required both the careful preservation of the existing structure and the restoration of missing components. An architectural model of the original was created for their reconstruction on the SIVA campus. The houses were first carefully dismantled from the original place, and the core timber frames numbered and packed one by one. During this process, the timber frame was rebuilt on a newly made reinforced concrete foundation. To guarantee structural safety, the load of all new roofs was taken up by the brick-concrete

The computer aided structural analysis of the original Lin ancient dwelling

The sitting room of Xu ancient dwelling; before and after relocation

Localization via dynamic behavioral expression

In these adaptive reuse cases, the essential architectural narrative symbols, such as wood structures and carved artifacts, can be preserved and passed down through the process of the migration. But these scattered Huizhou houses, far away from their hometown, are like the stray wild geese, having lost the beauty of the village community through their separation from original environments and historical contexts. The original nostalgic cultural memory carried by them will inevitably be lost and partially alienated during the reconstruction process. From the perspective of the immovability of architectural relics, the migration of heritage buildings is regrettable. As the rescue of non-protected old houses through relocation and reuse, the unique value lies in the localization of architectural culture in which an original living narrative of the building is integrated with a secondary narrative. Such a story is continued by various designers and users. Its dual narrative semantics reconstruct the new spatial experience of ancient dwellings and reflect human life in both modern and contemporary China. From the perspective of spatial behavior organization, space is not a container of invariable behavior, but a place of dynamic behavioral expression.[3]

Fortunately, the cases of these ancient dwellings at PEM, SIVA & SUTD have all been favorably received and the precious architectural heritage is further appreciated. Innovative migration and reconstruction have endowed traditional dwellings with a new life force, widely spreading the architectural culture originally confined to a certain area. But the three cases are very different. The core value of Yin Yu Tang is the static reappearance of original Chinese countryside home life in the form of a special museum exhibition. This translocation project received strong support from the department of cultural relics protection of Xiuning Count before the migration, with a signed cultural exchange agreement. The Chinese local government hoped to improve the international visibility of the Huizhou architectural culture with the help of American cultural institutions. It turned out to be a big success as seen in the endless streams of visitors and researchers who have gained an immersive experience of the Huizhou culture of China in Yin Yu Tang and a deeper understanding of life in a Chinese village of that time. With Yin Yu Tang as the base, the PEM often conducts a series of Chinese cultural exhibitions.

In the cases of SIVA & SUTD, the relocations fused functional aspects of the traditional dwellings with modern campus life. At SIVA, the Huizhou residential community, which was completed and opened in 2015, has not only become a living sample for teachers and students of Chinese wooden dwellings, but also a window for international visitors to understand Chinese traditional culture. Mrs. Shen Chen, from SIVA's School of New Media, has created a full-digital VR display design for the tea house. The user can realize remote immersive roaming with the help of the VR helmet, thus expanding the performance dimension of spatial cognition of the place. At SUTD, the four ancient structures have infused the modern campus with traditional Chinese customs. At the time of the transaction, there was some resistance to Jackie Chan gifting the houses to Singapore. The controversy dramatically increased the consensus of the importance of in-situ conservation of Chinese ancient buildings. With time, the SUTD case has gradually been accepted as that of a cultural ambassador rather than that of a loss of Chinese heritage. As Jackie Chan stated, "This is helpful to the world of cultural exchanges, it is hard to say only taking things back is patriotic. I have been committed to the promotion of Chinese culture overseas."[4] In both SIVA & SUTD, the vivid life of college staff and students continues the second narration of these ancient dwellings. In order to meet the requirement of teaching and research, both institutions have chosen innovative intervention and adaptive reuse instead of restoration as in the Yin Yu Tang of PEM. It is also due to the lack of historical archives that are needed for restoration, as these dwellings were hastily dismantled by someone else in the early years.

An antique Chinese pavilion on the campus of the Singapore University of Technology and Design

Conclusion

As a cultural phenomenon, the allopatric reconstruction of Huizhou ancient dwellings is driven by a number of reasons. While in-situ conservation is recommended for the protection of nostalgic culture, attention should be given to the new cultural value generated by ancient dwellings that have been relocated with the implantation of a secondary narrative. This value is reflected not only in the new spatial experience of the ancient dwellings, reconstructed by double narrative semantics, but also in the external communication of the local architectural culture in the context of globalization. In the life cycle of ancient dwellings, allopatric adaptive reuse has enriched the narrative connotations of the architecture across different dimensions.

ENDNOTES:

1 https://yinyutang.pem.org/

2 Shaoming Lu, "The origin of architectural narratology," *Journal of Tongji University* (social science edition), no.5(2012): 25–31.

3 Ropo A,Höykinpuro R, "Narrating Organizational Spaces," *Journal of Organizational Change Management*, no.30 (2017): 357–366.

4 Jackie Chan, Interview by Yansong Bai, *News 1+1*, Talk show of CCTV, Beijing, May 10,2013

The dismantled houses in storage at a Shanghai warehouse

INTERSTITIAL PRACTICES

THE STRATEGY OF THE IN-BETWEEN

by MADALINA GHIBUSI, JACOPO LEVERATTO[1]

In search of interstitial place-making

During the second half of the last century, public space design has gradually moved towards the center of the architectural debate, increasingly focused on improving urban liveability.[2] An improved understanding of urban design and the everyday use of public space within cities has become a fundamental parameter, and resilience has become an important aspect for managing the transformations of contemporary cities. With the world population having doubled in the last fifty years, and two thirds of all people believed to relocate to urban areas by the middle of this century, the awareness for open and inclusive public spaces has became an essential factor for the development of more sustainable and resilient urban societies.[3] By consequence, the definition of a city has begun to require a total rethinking of its traditional use and meaning, demanding new forms of place-making.

A strong impulse in this direction has started to emerge over the last twenty years, with studies and design experimentations about the re-activation of urban interstices, resulting as a leftover after a central planning process, or between two heterogeneous and discontinuous actions.[4] Urban interstices are small *in-between* spaces in the urban built environment, such as vacant lots, unused infrastructural pertinences, or abandoned green spaces. Their lack of formal identity, reflected in the past a lack of public interest or collective engagement, often ended up defining exclusionary spaces for minority populations.[5] Although they could be seen as a failure of urban development or

"Casa do Quarteirão" (Ponta Delgada, Açores, 2016), a participatory project
of public space reactivation, initiated by the Italian group Orizzontale
within the framework of Walk&Talk Festival 2016.
Photo courtesy of Orizzontale.

"Casa do Quarteirão," the participatory construction process.
Photo courtesy of Orizzontale.

even as the prototype of "anti-public space,"[6] they also showed the remarkable potential of non-prescriptive spaces, liable to a continuous redefinition of social roles and values. For this reason, they have not only been studied as places of social exclusion, but also as possible incubators for experimenting with new practices of public citizenship beyond a merely commercial perspective.[7] In other words, both from a social and spatial point of view, urban interstices have gradually emerged as a central but marginalized asset, which could be used to explore new forms of collective participation and public engagement. This implies the necessity of defining new tools and methodologies of re-activation capable of building a new sense of community around the everyday practices of spatial production.[8]

While attempts are still being made at municipal and regional planning, top-down actions of urban design and management have gradually receded.[9] As cities have become more dense and their functional programs more variable, smaller urban catalysts have pervasively become a preferred mode of intervention for public space-building and activation.[10] These "tactical" modes of intervention have arisen as a counterpart to a classic and strategic notion of planning and are executed in the form of everyday and bottom-up approaches to local problems, which make use of short-term, low-cost and scalable interventions and policies.[11] Whether they have been sanctioned or not by urban authorities, they represent a creative re-appropriation of the contemporary city's public dimension, in an uncoordinated form of domestication.

This has meant a significant change in scale, from macro to micro, and a new way of looking at the morphogenetic mechanisms of urban projects, from a series of sequential operations to a simultaneous process in which various decisional agents interact to generate a complex spatial system.[12] Moreover, it has shifted the conceptual core of public space design from a purely spatial dimension to a multi-layered one, which has also been made of immaterial factors such as participatory processes, communication projects, consensus building mechanisms, specific regulations and conditions of use.[13] In summary, the emerging attempts of tactical urbanism have been challenging both the traditional parameters of public space design and the role of planners, architects, and other urban practitioners, thus requiring new strategies that effectively mix top-down and bottom-up impulses. This design approach can be achieved by selecting, coordinating and managing heterogeneous, multidisciplinary and multi-scale design contributions, in an *in-between design approach* that is still in search of a clear definition.

One problem with an alternative design approach is that top-down and bottom-up processes of place-making are not comparable, and their activation requires a differentiated set of tools and methodologies. Top-down approaches involve academic institutions, associations, municipality and other authorities in a multidisciplinary, inter-institutional project. Bottom-up processes place meanings on connections made through reciprocity.[14] In other words, when managing the regeneration of a complex territory from a top-down point of view, participation is obtained through procedures that involve the development of a network characterized by a significant autonomy and clarity in roles. Bottom-up approaches use spontaneous forms of activation, in which stories play a fundamental role in how people assign value to a place and to an action. They are still not well known and need further definition, as new design approaches to identify best practices of this spontaneous activity across different contexts increase.

In between top-down and bottom-up.

In the postwar period, the human scale approach initiated by Team 10 was a critique of the urban design promoted inside the CIAM Congresses. This critique evolved into a tension between the street level perspective and the birds-eye one, between starting from a *tabula rasa* or from the social context, and between the structured and the sensitive. In other words, there was a clear segregation between the bottom-up and the top-down approach.

The urban realities of today push towards a more flexible approach "moving away from top-down, large-scale masterplanning, to a much more strategic and sensitive planning,"[15] that allows the development of research processes essential to the understanding of the complex contemporary city. Fredericks, Caldwell and Tomitsch refer to "middle-out design,"[16] advocating against the traditional categorizations of top-down and bottom-up and proposing "that both decision makers and local communities should be involved in the city making process."[17] This flexible approach is also increasingly sustained by the previously skeptical municipalities that are becoming "more open and receptive to listening and understanding the needs of the public domain, and are now aiding in the emergence of those initiatives."[18] This role of municipality as facilitator is crucial to this kind of process, as it can enable and continuously restructure the fragile and subjective micro entities that build the process from the bottom.

Therefore, the projects that manage to adapt to the current urban complexity are the ones that mitigate the two opposed notions in an *in-between* approach that entail tools able to calibrate the movement between the two extremes, between different tactics and strategies, arriving to a more curatorial approach of the process of intervention in the contemporary space. Such interventions are developed throughout Europe by multidisciplinary collectives such as StudioBASAR, Orizzontale, Basurama, Collectif Etc, Atelier D'architecture Autogérée, etc.

In between public and private

The *in-between* of public and private can be both the characteristic of the socio-spatial reality and of the physical host. Herman Hertzberger proposed the concept of *in-between* as the "key to eliminating the sharp division between areas with different territorial claims."[19] This *in-between* assumes the role of the public-private negotiators that "establish the two extremes of a sliding scale in degrees of publicness, where overlaps rather than strict boundaries mark transition zones."[20] The *in-between* public and private is becoming the main characteristic of the contemporary public space in the context of a growing domestication of the public domain: "the privatization occurs both in the sense of personalizing a portion of public space by regular use and in the sense of learning how to manage one's body to create a symbolic shield of privacy in public."[21] This reality is materialized, for example, by the Caseando project in Madrid: "A new collective space, distributed in a network of domestic practices[22] and generates new areas or fields based on openess." [23]

The *in-between* public and private is also found in the *in-between* space as it is showcased by Alan Thomas, who presents the urban environment of Japan through a photographic documentation that is centered on the *in-between* spaces, with their narrow character and their abundance of small-scale but innovative improvisations that show their malleability in a very constrained context: "These minor spaces are at once public and oddly intimate."[24] This subjective peculiarity is possible as the "in between spaces are invested with desires and imagined (not imaginary) needs."[25] Therefore, the *in-between*, in this context, reveals itself through the feeling that these spaces of no one are actually spaces for everyone.

In between formal and informal. In between soft and hard

The current situation of the urban tissue reveals how intensive urban growth has led to an archipelago of hybridizations. This condition embeds several tensions between the formal and informal settings as the city functions through a continuous flow of usage that evolves both in the built and unbuilt space, both in the planned and non-planned areas. This form of space is lately more researched[26] and recognized by several common characteristics that are identifiable in the relationship between the formal and informal: "In this connection it is important to emphasise that it is not the single formal or informal processes that determine the positive outcome of the planning and design process for urban space, but rather the quality of the relations existing between the two spatial concepts. The informal, placing itself in a dialectical relation with the formal, configures relational spaces and defines a meeting point between two different ways of structuring

society."[27] This meeting point is where the *in-between* notion is placed and from where, once again, it can shift in one direction or the other, revealing the existing and adapting it to future possibilities. Several opportunities can be identified: "to withdraw from the formal and informal control of public space to a less controlled territory"[28] which can be called the *in-between* territory. This territory between soft and hard, or between formal and informal is formulated by Peter Eisenman as the relationship between *topos* and *atopos*, or "to be between some place and no place."[29] From this perspective, the *in-between* can range from formal and informal spaces (the "hard") to formal and informal practices (the "soft"). An example of *in-between* soft and hard can be found in the French city Rennes, where The Hotel Pasteur project is planning on opening to the public without any predefined program. The only condition is that actions must last from one hour to up to three months in this space, and leave some trace after they end. So this type of program is the "soft" component that is enabling and further developing a pre-existing structure. This "hard" permanent structure is reappropriated through "soft" temporary actions revealing another calibrating aspect of the notion of *in-between*: the one between temporary and permanent. Therefore, *in-between* soft and hard, *in-between* the formal and informal, and *in-between* temporary and permanent are actually the peculiar binom of a productive collision between several opposed realities.

Conclusion

Since its first formulation,[30] the concept of *in-betweenness* has accumulated many different meanings, to reach a level at which it can speak about the production of the contemporary city from very different perspectives. Today, in fact, although the term is still used to indicate the spatial condition that characterizes urban interstices, it mainly connotes a multilayered set of strategies that distinguish the process of their reactivation. This is because, unlike interstitiality, in-betweenness does not refer to a specific typological domain, but rather to a topological one. This is to say that, whereas the former refers to some spatial categories that are established within the field of design, the latter has to do with a very different state that does not involve a particular shape, but is determined by some qualitative properties that spatially translate some persisting logical relations. Thus, the term can be used both to describe a spatial condition and the logical relations that define a relational and dialogical field between diverse and autonomous entitities.

ENDNOTES:

1 Jacopo Leveratto is the author of the first and the last paragraphs, while Madalina Ghibusi is the author of the three central ones.

2 Matthew Carmona, *Public Places-Urban Spaces: The Dimensions of Urban Design* (Oxford: Elsevier, 2003).

3 Pedro Gadanho ed., *Uneven Growth: Tactical Urbanisms for Expanding Megacities* (New York: MoMA, 2014).

4 Andrea Brighenti ed., *Urban Interstices: The Aesthetics and the Politics of the In-between* (London: Routledge, 2013).

5 Don Mitchell, *The Right to the City: Social Justice and the Fight for Public Space* (New York: Guilford, 2003); Peter Marcuse, "From Critical Urban Theory to the Right to the City," *City*, no. 13 (2009): 185-197.

6 Jean-François Chevrier, *Des Territoires* (Paris: L'Arachnéen, 2011).

7 Gil Doron, "The Dead Zone and the Architecture of Transgression," *City,* no. 4 (2000): 247-263.

8 Jacopo Leveratto, "Planned To Be Reclaimed: Public Design Strategies for Spontaneous Practices of Spatial Appropriation," *Street Art & Urban Creativity Scientific Journal*, no. 1 (2015): 6-12.

9 Gadanho, *Uneven Growth*.

10 Jaime Lerner, *Urban Acupuncture* (Washington: Island Press, 2016).

11 Mike Lydon and Anthony Garcia, *Tactical Urbanism: Short-term Action for Long-term Change* (Washington: Island Press, 2015).

12 Robert Klanten and Martin Hubner, *Urban Interventions: Personal Projects in Public Spaces* (Berlin: Gestalten, 2010).

13 Janette Sadik-Khan, *Streetfight: Handbook for an Urban Revolution* (New York: Viking, 2016).

14 Gabrielle Bendiner-Viani, "The Big World in the Small: Layered Dynamics of Meaning-making in the Everyday," *Environment and Planning D: Society and Space* 31, no. 4 (2013): 708-726.

15 Jeroen Zuidgeest, in *Re-Act: Tools for Urban Re-Activation*, ed. Gianpiero Venturini and Carlo Venegoni (Roma/Rezzato: Deleyva Editore, 2016), 33.

16 Joel Fredericks, Glenda Amayo Caldwell and Martin Tomitsch, "Middle-out design: collaborative community engagement in urban HCI," in *Proceedings of the 28th Australian Conference on Computer-Human Interaction* (Launceston, TAS: ACM), 200.

17 Joel Fredericks, Glenda Amayo Caldwell and Martin Tomitsch, "Middle-out design: collaborative community engagement in urban HCI," in *Proceedings of the 28th Australian Conference on Computer-Human Interaction* (Launceston: ACM), 200.

18 Gianpiero Venturini and Carlo Venegoni, *Re-Act: Tools for Urban Re-Activation* (Roma/Rezzato: Deleyva Editore, 2016), 17.

19 Herman Hertzberger, *Lessons for Students in Architecture* (Rotterdam: 010 Publishers, 2005), 40.

20 Helena Piha, "Making Public Space. About the Same or About Difference?," *The Journal of Public Space* 2, no. 2 (2017): 155.

21 Mark Chidister, "Public Places, Private Life: Plazas and the Broader Public," *Places* 6, no. 1 (1989): 35.

22 This refers to the 'personal dimension' (Venturini and Venegoni 2016) of certain practices, like the projects and initiatives focusing on the private rather than the public. The idea is that placing a public initiative like Caseandoin the context of private projects (like housing), is creating a system of new relations between public and private, that require an open attitude to these changes. This system is the new reality of the collective areas of the city that incorporate these zones of 'in-between public and private'.

23 Gianpiero Venturini and Carlo Venegoni, *Re-Act: Tools for Urban Re-Activation* (Roma/Rezzato: Deleyva Editore, 2016), 46.

24 Alan Thomas, "Open Secrets," *Places Journal*, (March 2010).

25 Andrea Brighenti, ed., *Urban Interstices: The Aesthetics and the Politics of the In-between* (London: Routledge, 2013), XIX.

26 Giovanna Piccinno and Elisa Lega (2012) and Gianpaola Spirito (2015) are referring to several spatial and social phenomena through the notion of in-between, always emphasizing the emergence of this type of space in the second half of the past century until present as a consequence of the surrounding contexts, from global to local scale.

27 Laura Lutzoni, "In-formalized Urban Space Design. Rethinking the Relationship between Formal and Informal," *City*, Territory and Architecture 3, no. 20 (2016): 10.

28 Tomas Wikström, "Residual space and transgressive spatial practices – the uses and meanings of un-formed space," *Nordisk arkitekturforskning* 18, no. 1 (2005): 54.

29 Peter Eisenman, "Blue Line Text," In *Postmodernism: Critical Concepts* Vol. IV, ed. Viktor E. Taylor and Charles E. Winquist (London: Routledge, 1998): 356.

30 Martin Buber, "Das problem des Menschen (1943)," *Forum*, no. 8 (1959): 24; Aldo van Eyck, "Dutch Forum on Children's Home," *Forum*, no. 32 (1962): 602.

Fabien (at the age of twelve), *untitled*, acrylic on kraft paper, 183 x 99 cm.

IN SEARCH OF SPATIAL NARRATIVES

by ANDREAS MÜLLER

The call for spatial narratives was just too appealing, all the more for a dilettante in matters spatial. On the vague terrain prepared by the uncertain constellations between the two terms involved, I chose to make 'narrative space' into a standpoint from which to explore the potentials of reflecting about what is in search here – taking for a maxim that the truth of an understanding proves itself in what you can do with it.

Starting by doing away with some possibilities, the "spirited spin through history" characteristic of rather post-modern approaches to *Narrative Architecture*[1] will not come into consideration here. Much more must be said about the reasons for which I do not pursue three other and immediately evident approaches to narrative space, namely via the narrative, via space and via narrative space. "Narrative space"[2] was used as a title, and possibly coined as a term,[3] by literary theoretician and film critic Stephen Heath in a 1976 article dedicated to the narrative space of film, an article worth reading for many thoughts very close to our concerns – including the welcome booty of a quotation from Merleau-Ponty "that 'the aspect of the world would be transformed if we succeeded in seeing as things the intervals between things.'" Yet even with film having penetrated life in the course of the four decades since, film is always much

concerned with its own ways as a specific medium. The transition from one medium's cosmos to the other, there's the rub, and one that seems not to have been mastered yet between architecture and film.

Space, more surprisingly, does not seem either to lend itself for an approach to narrative spaces – space, a term that has become so dear to architects in the last 120 years or so[4] that one may consider as *communis opinio* that making architecture is making spaces.[5] It may come as somewhat disillusioning that among the articles in the *Encyclopædia Britannica* carrying "space" as the sole or main term in their titles there are physics, metaphysics, mathematics, biology and psychology (with topology delicately ranged with mathematics), while one has to dive into the recesses of "Architecture," category "Expression," subcategory "Form" in order to emerge with the first paragraphs of the sub-subcategory "Space and mass."[6] I would venture that this may come less from an obsolete conservatism of the medium or society and more from the character of architectural design, core competency of the discipline and the profession of architecture: its character of integrating the knowledge, resources and competencies of a wide range of other disciplines and professions. But then, if integration it is, what are the specific abilities that fulfil the condition of possibility to integrate the physical, geometrical, geographical, infrastructural, social, psychological, et cetera, spaces by means of architectural spaces?

Now it may have been to consider too curiously, to consider so. Narrative spaces, before all, are meant to tell stories[7] and it is certainly not necessary to reflect about what a narrative is or what a space is for telling and hearing stories in spaces. Hearing ... well, reading ... ok, seeing ... well just intuitively grasping the meaning ... oh dear. – While it seems possible to analyze the means and methods of spaces in paintings that are narrative by intention or convention, [8] and while there are attempts at understanding or creating built interior spaces according to patterns and strategies of dramatic development[9] or at understanding the architectural settings in literary narrative texts as means and methods to develop mental interior spaces[10] – there is, it seems, by contrast, no conceptual understanding of means and methods of telling stories by architectural spaces.

This is a bold and rather nonchalantly introduced assumption and I hasten to put it in its place. Each and every architectural design that lends a presence to a past, or that represents a building's context in a building, or that expresses a notion in its forms, or that embodies a type in its individuality, uses means and methods to convey what it openly or subliminally strives to convey. There are signs and symbols, metaphors and metonymies, examples and partes pro toto, lieutenants and other representatives, oppositions and articulations and insinuations and slurrings and so many more ways of saying that a concept, a space, a shape, an element, something that is there or is not there means something that is not there but is meant to be there. But – no matter whether it is Scarpa in Venice or Eisenman in Columbus or Libeskind in Berlin or Hariri in Santiago or the unknown architect's densification of social housing in anywhere of all places – certainly we understand what it is meant to mean and in the fortunate case it is beautiful, appropriate and lively, a success – yet, still, there may be a lingering, an eerie je-ne-sais-quoi of: I do not fully understand; I like it, but if another person does not like it, what can I say?

What I would like to suggest is to conceptually understand architecturally designed narrative spaces as images. Or to put it more bluntly for a point of departure: to understand architecture as an image. Of course, the value of this proposition, whether it is banal and a humbug or whether it is not, depends entirely on what is meant here by image. As the fields of meanings of 'image' are so immensely rich, wide and diverse, it is not an option to sort out from the available discourses what is meant here and what not. So the following can by no means do justice to the works or even thoughts referred to.

Was ist ein Bild?[11] "What is an image?" is the title of a book edited by eminent German art historian Gottfried Boehm, a collection of articles revolving around that question. In the first place, he argues with fresh directness, and on the basis that "Bild" can be used for image, picture and painting alike, an image is something that has a frame.[12] The frame, by isolating the image from the other things around it, indicates two essential features of an image: it indicates that this is an image, i.e. something other than the other things that are not images; and it states that everything that is in the picture, so to speak, belongs, is probably by intention and certainly by fact part of the image. So the image is an entity, an individuum, and one that is different from the non-images.

Proceeding from these basics, what then distinguishes an image from non-images? It was made to be looked at, and it contains what is meant to be looked at. Some spontaneous examples to make this more clear: If something that functions as a frame were installed high up the Centre Pompidou through which onlookers would catch glances at segments of the city, even this would be an image, an image made out of air and light, constituted as an image by the frame and containing what the beholder sees on the plane defined by the frame. By contrast, a shard glazed in a specific color that a ceramics manufacturer retains at the end of a commission as the only way to identify and recreate the same color later, would not be an image, no matter the aesthetic qualities it may have, no matter that it needs to be looked at and that it fully contains what is meant to be looked at – because 'it has no frame.'

Another aspect of an image is that, being made, it is made of something, which makes it some thing among the other things. As everything here, this is meant with more than a grain of salt. To the same extent as a sculpture whose concept comprises its being invisibly buried in the ground, is and remains an image in the understanding promoted here, the mental image may also figure as an image in this sense – if, and this is important, it materializes, becomes constant enough and defined enough to be mentally perceived as an image, at some distance (as sight is a sense of distance) by the inner eye – if, in short, it gains object-like qualities, qualities inimitably caught in the German term "Gegenstand"[13] with its allusions to opposition and physical robustness.

We are now at the point where the preceding efforts of conception are expected to bear fruit. An image is an object that shows something; it has a presence and represents something. What it represents is there, because it is in the picture, and at the same time it is not there, because what is there is only the image. An immense intellectual struggle was fought during millennia over this phenomenon of a simultaneous presence and absence in representations,[14] and while this phenomenon is difficult to describe in common language without resorting to the doubtful word 'ambivalence,' Gottfried Boehm is considered to have thoroughly addressed it in

Fabien (at the age of thirteen), *untitled*, acrylic on kraft paper, 171,5 x 98,5 cm.

Fabien (at the age of thirteen), *untitled*, acrylic on kraft paper, 162 x 96 cm.

the newly defined field of image studies ("*Bildwissen-schaft*") and named it "iconic difference": the image-inherent difference between the representation and what is represented.

The present plea for understanding architecture as an image is based on two supposed features of this iconic difference: that it is constituent for an image, and that it is a good thing, too. No surprise, both these assumptions have been radically contested. In architecture, in a statement on their Blur Building for the Swiss Expo 2002, Diller + Scofidio claim that its understanding "must be liberated from all immediate and obvious metaphoric associations such as clouds, god, angels, ascension, dreams, Greek mythology, or any other kitsch relationship."[15] I would critically argue that this statement is mixing up issues in image, metaphor and relationship and I do not believe that it is possible to look at a design like this without being bothered by the inherent iconic difference.

Their statement also implies the other fundamental imputation against the iconic difference: namely that it be dissolved, i.e., that its two sides, what is 'really present' and what is 'only meant,' engage in a sort of reconciling inventory of what is here and what is there, with an artful interplay between the two sides as the most to be gained, and with a unity as result. I think, by contrast, that the concept of iconic difference comprises an entirely different intellectual topos. It is a topos similar to philosopher Niklas Luhmann's thought[16] that morals, i.e. the enactment of the difference between overarching norms and individual acts, usually understood to aim at a harmonization between the two sides involved, are instead a system enabling a sustainable process of disagreement. In the same vein, also Luhmann, trust, usually understood as a method to overcome the threatening difference between a promise and an act, be instead a strategy of handling this – insuperable – difference. On another field, one that may be closer to our concerns, the imaginative way in which a metaphor creates new meaning, by likeness and assimilation in popular belief, is understood by philosopher Paul Ricœur, by contrast, as a process "not above the differences ... but in spite of and through the differences;" "caught in the war between distance and proximity, between remoteness and nearness" of the elements involved in a metaphor.[17] In this spirit and in this sense, we must imagine the iconic difference unreconciled – but mediated in and by the image.

Now in architecture, it is more than plain that there are conflicting oppositions unreconciled to some extent – if not to that reflected in Samuel Beckett's suggestions for the exchange of insults between Vladimir and Estragon: "V. Andouille/E. Tordu/V. Crétin./E. Curé./V. Dégueulasse/E. Micheton/V. Ordure/E. architecte."[18] But can, and should, oppositions in architecture be understood as difference between what is there as a presence and what is there as an absence; and can, and should, this difference be understood as being an iconic difference of an image, i.e. a difference in, and mediated by, an entity 'that has a frame,' meant to be looked at and representing something else?

In lieu of a coherent discussion, let me refer to three idiosyncratic examples as a test. First, entering today the town hall of Kalk, Cologne, Germany, designed by the other Gottfried Böhm[19] in the year when he received the Pritzker Prize, 1986, I found myself in a maze of confusingly semi-open, uncertainly shaped spaces, walkways and corridors with a correspondingly heterogeneous mix of materials and formal gestures. At a minimum I should think that this is so 80s or less placidly, that this is ugly and bad architecture. But I don't, and I suspect for the reason not of genius or importance but because this questionable shape is strongly pervaded by the presence of what it means; or more exactly, by the presence of *that* it means: because its meanings (presumably in terms of contextual reference, historical transformation and societal vision) are far from being concretely there, but it is all the more present that they are meant, whatever they are. It is this quality, the ability of making present what is absent, that makes the difference, the iconic difference, I presume.

Secondly, Santiago Calatrava's Oculus building for the World Trade Center transportation hub would be a case in point to argue that the said difference is, at best, a limited special case. No difference here, one should think: it's meant to soar and it soars. The statement it makes and the physical presence it takes may both be debatable and they have been debated, but that's beside the point here; the point is that, if one likes both the statement and the shape, there still remains a friction inherent in this design as being undisputedly a built metaphor. Regarding it as an image, I suggest, instead of a metaphor may allow new viewpoints for fruitful criticism. For instance, referring to the building's sculptural quality, a sculpture, understood as a kind of image, would be questioned regarding its ways of combining the factual and the fictional, of transforming its bodily subject into a work.[20] Or a metaphor, understood as part of an image, would be questioned about the ways in which it processes the recombination of the two likened elements, and makes the processing visible, within this frame.

Thirdly, look at any building designed in the spirit and with the means of 'evidence-based design' – "the conscientious, explicit, and judicious use of current best evidence from research and practice in making critical decisions ... about the design of each individual and unique project"[21] – and consider to what extent and in what ways the resulting building deals with meaning.

Coming back from here to the initial and more specific proposition of conceptually understanding architecturally designed *spaces* as images, I would like to refer to the endeavors of architectural theorist Philippe Boudon. He considers architecture's potential as an epistemological field of its own right, say like chemistry or linguistics, so when he writes "On Architectural Space"[22] he writes about the very particular space in which the architectural designer performs his operations. Interestingly in our context, he understands this space as consisting of, and mediating between, two very different spaces: the mental space of the designer and the real space of our world; and he understands the relation between these two spaces not in terms of any sequence in a process, but as a conceptual whole, in which the mental space is being *represented* in the real space. Boudon's understanding of representation is not, as he emphasizes, as "furiously pictorial" as Erwin Panofsky's, who looks at an architectural space like at a painting. Far from it, the real space of our world consists of so many dimensions beyond the scope of architecture, and at the other end, the mental space is far from containing 'the real thing' ready to be implemented. What happens in architecture (at this point and in this understanding of architecture as an art of representation in real space) is that the representation of mental space in real space leads to the emergence of an architectural space, which, being created by design, appears as a whole and which, appearing as a whole and containing a representational relationship between what is there and what is meant, can be seen as an image.

This point of view opens up innumerable ways of understanding. Boudon, for one, calls for a "semiotic investigation" of the images in architecture, which "does not make the mistake to reduce the image to what can be said."[23] Peter Eisenman, in Kurt Forster's understanding, thought that what makes a post a post, in architecture, is its dual existence as a post and a sign of a post," so that "a post is not a post without assuming its role as a signpost..."[24] Perspectival projection, usually understood as an invention extending the grip on the real world, may by contrast be seen as an extension of the means to represent mental spaces, namely by making use of the real world as an image (and, in particular, by involving the beholder's perspective in the image).[25] William Kentridge, considering how to convey his narrative about the African porters in WW1 in the representation of his art on the large stage of *The Head and the Load* in the vast main hall of Park Avenue Armory, among other places, wished that the representational relationship be "revelatory rather than explanatory."[26] We could take a new look at spatial narratives from here.

I would like to end with a story about the creation of narrative spaces by a series of images. Looking at them may reverberate, in many ways, with much of what was brought up here. The three paintings shown here, in acrylic on kraft paper, are by a boy called Fabien by psychiatrist, filmmaker and painter Alain Gillis, in the book *Le Bazar du Génie*.[27] Fabien had lived for a couple of years in Gillis' psychotherapeutic institution because he was unable to relate to the world and to other people or, as Gillis puts it, "he found himself situated in a peculiar way," in a "particular relation of his being to space and to the world," namely one that was, in one word, limitless. Among many utensils offered to him *ad libitum*, without any art therapy, were those for painting, and Fabien resorted to them following a form of treatment that consisted of packing him tightly in lukewarm blankets and considering together with him the "elementary spatio-temporal constituents" of this experience. The first painting shown here was among the first of some three hundred that Fabien created over more than two years when he was eleven, twelve and thirteen. It shows, says Gillis, "the imperative that space be eventually constituted as a complete and limited object," as defined, unified and continuous – in an attempt "to bring an end to a space without difference, that holds the subject in an impossible situation, 'beside himself'." Still, it is the image of a space in which the author does not figure. The other two paintings were created within few days toward the end of this creative period, and now, in the second painting shown here, the painter is in – only to go out, in the third of these paintings, in the form of a number of viewpoints, into a space which can now be allowed to be undivided – the whole arrangement clearly mediated by the frame of the image.

Gillis emphasizes that these paintings, driven by a natural *souci* and lacking any freedom of and in communication with others, are not yet works of art. But they are also no longer natural objects, because the necessity driving their creation is "the necessity of an immediate and directed view that sustains the *being*, that responds to him in a helpful way. The painting's ... organization is the capital expression of a single meaning. The sign that the meaning *is*." – Gillis ends by telling that Fabien painted less and less. "*Il préfère jardiner*."

ENDNOTES:

1 Nigel Coates, *Narrative Architecture*. AD Primers (Chichester: John Wiley and Sons, 2012). The quotation is from a review of this book by Jonathan Glancey, "Coates of Many Colours," *Architectural Review*, 27 March 2012, retrieved from architectural-review.com.

2 Stephen Heath, "Narrative Space," *Screen*, vol. 17, issue 3 (1 October 1976), pp. 68-112. The subsequent quotation from Merleau-Ponty is on p. 107 and is referenced to his article "Le cinéma et la nouvelle psychologie," in Merleau-Ponty, *Sens et non-sens* (Paris, 1948), p. 110, evidently translated here by Heath.

3 According to artist Mia Zona in her Blog mineofgod.wordpress.com in the one month of its activity, January 2014.

4 The lecture and subsequent book by August Schmarsow, *Das Wesen der architektonischen Schöpfung*, in which he introduced the novel idea of architecture as "*Raumgestalterin*" ("shaper of space"), date from 1893 and 1894 respectively. On this context see Mitchell W. Schwarzer, "The Emergence of Architectural Space: August Schmarsow's Theory of 'Raumgestaltung,'" *Assemblage*, no. 15 (Aug. 1991), pp. 48-61.

5 For example, Louis Kahn, "Architecture is the thoughtful making of spaces," *Perspecta*, vol. 4 (1957), pp. 2-3.

6 James S. Ackerman, Roger Scruton, Peter Collins, Alan Gowans, "Architecture," in *Encyclopædia Britannica*, article published 23 August 2018, retrieved from britannica.com. Truly the French counterpart, *Encyclopædia Universalis*, offers a 19-page article by Jean Guiraud and Françoise Choay, "Espace, architecture et esthétique." But then in the three volumes of the German *Enzyklopädie Philosophie* with the fine provenance of Felix Meiner Verlag, Hamburg, 2010, the article by Manfred Stöckler on "Raum" mentions this subject as relevant for architecture only very marginally with regard to the organization and experience of spaces. And the very topical *Lexikon Raumphilosophie*, ed. Stephan Güntzel (Darmstadt: Wissenschaftliche Buchgesellschaft, 2012), does without an article on architecture.

7 See, for example, the Bartlett Narrative/Making/Space team reporting on their PhD activities on https://www.ucl.ac.uk/bartlett/news/2017/dec/making-spaces-meaningful-through-architectural-storytelling.

8 A leading advocate of this approach to paintings is art historian Wolfgang Kemp, who applied this approach in his book *Die Räume der Maler. Zur Bilderzählung seit Giotto* (Munich: Beck, 1996) and published an introduction to his approach, "Narrative," in Robert S. Nelson (ed.), *Critical Terms for Art History*. Chicago: University of Chicago Press, 1996), pp. 58-69.

9 Architect Holger Kleine has developed fundamentals of "spatial dramaturgy" in his book *The Drama of Space. Spatial Sequences and Compositions in Architecture* (Basel: Birkhäuser, 2017).

10 For example, Julia Weber's topical research at the Peter Szondi Institut of Comparative Literature at Freie Universität Berlin.

11 Gottfried Boehm (ed.), *Was ist ein Bild?* (Munich: Wilhelm Fink Verlag, 1994). Even though Boehm initiated and inspired a wealth of international research, hardly any of his numerous publications are available in English. A glimpse may be caught in Boehm's article "Representation, Presentation, Presence: Tracing the Homo Pictor," transl. Julia Sonnevend and Dominik Bartmanski, in Jeffrey C. Alexander, Dominik Bartmanski, Bernhard Giesen (eds.), *Iconic Power. Materiality and Meaning in Social Life* (New York: Palgrave Macmillan, 2012), pp. 15-24. There is an extensive account on the contents of *Was ist ein Bild?* in the review by Stefan Beyst, "Gottfried Boehm and the image," dated March 2010 and published online at d-sites.net/english/boehm.html.

12 The term "frame" is mine; it is a pointed emphasis of the following: "What we encounter as an image is based on a single fundamental contrast, the one between a contained overall surface and what it contains in terms of internal events." From Boehm, "Die Wiederkehr der Bilder," chapter "V. Die ikonische Differenz," in Boehm, *Was ist ein Bild?*, pp. 29-30.

13 *Gegenstand* seems to have been created only in the 18th century as a German loan translation for *object*, carrying a stronger flair of counter (*gegen*) and upright (*stand*).

14 A particularly endearing manifestation of this debate is the dialogue between poet Yves Bonnefoy and doctor and literary scholar Jean Starobinski, "Fonctions de l'Image," at Université de Nice, 1975, published on Youtube by Éclair brut.

15 Diller & Scofidio, *Blur: the making of nothing* (New York: Harry N. Abrams, 2002), p. 325. This publication was followed by an architectural monograph with a topical title: Edward Dimendberg, *Diller Scofidio + Renfro: Architecture after Images* (Chicago: University of Chicago Press, 2013).

16 Niklas Luhmann, "Soziologie der Moral," in Niklas Luhmann und Stephan H. Pfürtner, *Theorietechnik und Moral* (Frankfurt on Main: Suhrkamp, 1978), pp. 8-116; there seems to be no published English translation. Niklas Luhmann, *Vertrauen* (Stuttgart: Enke, 1968), was published in English as part of Luhmann, *Trust and Power* (New York: John Wiley and Sons, 1979), transl. Howard Davies, John Raffan and Kathryn Rooney.

17 Paul Ricœur, "The Metaphorical Process as Cognition, Imagination, and Feeling," *Critical Inquiry*, vol. 5, no. 1, (Special Issue on Metaphor, Autumn 1978), pp. 143-159, quotation on pp. 148-149.

18 Hand-written addition by Beckett on p. 127 of his personal copy of *En Attendant Godot*, shown and put into context on the website of Trinity College Dublin, https://www.tcd.ie/trinitywriters/writers/samuel-beckett/.

19 Gottfried Böhm is a German architect, born in 1920, not cousin to Gottfried Boehm.

20 On sculpture understood as a spatial image see the article by Gundolf Winter, "Bild – Raum – Raumbild. Zum Phänomen dreidimensionaler Bildlichkeit," in Gundolf Winter, Jens Schröter, Joanna Barck (eds.), *Das Raumbild. Bilder jenseits ihrer Flächen* (Paderborn: Fink, 2009), pp. 47-63.

21 D. Kirk Hamilton, David H. Watkins, *Evidence-Based Design for Multiple Building Types* (Hoboken: John Wiley & Sons, 2008), p. 9.

22 Philippe Boudon, *Sur l'espace architectural* (Paris: Dunod, 1971). There is no published English translation. The quotation on Erwin Panofsky is on p.23. Boudon develops his understanding of architectural *Conception* (Paris: Éditions de La Villette, 2004) on the basis of a comparison of two images by Pablo Picasso and Joseph Jastrow.

23 Philippe Boudon, "Pas d'images(s) sans échelle(s)," in: Philippe Boudon (ed.), *Langages singuliers et partagés de l'architecture* (Paris: L'Harmattan, 2003), pp. 173-184, quotation on p. 181.

24 Kurt W. Forster in his laudatory speech for the honorary doctorate for Peter Eisenman, Technische Universität Berlin, 20 December 2018, published on YouTube by Institute für Architektur TU Berlin.

25 Leads in this direction may be found in the catalogue, published on YouTube by Institut für Architektur TU Berlin for the Renaissance exhibition in the Alte Pinakothek in Munich 2018: Andreas Schumacher (ed.), *Florence and its Painters. From Giotto to Leonardo da Vinci* (Munich: Hirmer, 2018).

26 William Kentridge in "Artist Talk: The Head & The Load," 6 December 2018, published on Youtube by Park Avenue Armory.

27 Alain Gillis, *Le Bazar du Génie. La pratique esthétique des enfants présentant des troubles de la communication* (Paris: Société Nouvelle Adam Biro and Association Documentation – Étude pour le Traitement des Troubles Autistiques, IME Montaigne, avenue de Turenne, 77500 Chelles, 2002). The quotations are on pp. 11, 32-37 and 110, the descriptions of the paintings on pp. 100-110 and the illustrations on pp. 112, 118 and 119.

LOOKING FROM THE VOIDS IN-BETWEEN

by GÉRALDINE BORIO

Behind the legitimate city, for which we can easily
draw the outlines, lies the city of "in-betweens," a city in
a constant state of transformation, but which inspires
precisely because it has not been finished or defined,
leaving room for the imagining of a future or a past. At a
macroscale, morphological "in-betweens" are identified
as industrial wastelands, infrastructure surroundings,
vacant plots, waste grounds; so-called "urban diseases"
resulting from deindustrialisation or territorial fragmentation pushed by economic agendas. At a microscale,
they are small gaps and recesses, resulting from the
mutational process of the built environment.

   For users, these areas in transition, abandoned, offer
a momentary space to appropriate. Motivated more by
pragmatism than sentimentalism or nostalgia, users of
in-betweens find a space that answers a need. Activities
taking place in these vacant lands are more or less legal,
but always temporary. The intensity of the appropriation
of voids is tightly linked to the extent of the repression
felt in the built, the planned, and the official surrounding
them. Yet, devoid of systematic functions, programmes,
and rules, in-betweens bring a feeling of liberation.
We feel free to interpret them.

A shoe maker located at the entrance of a back lane in Sham Shui Po

For an architect in search of a territory for action, these sites represent an opportunity to intervene. Without the need to leave a physical imprint, one can imagine strategies for recreating relationships—between people, between sites, between people and sites—turning the negative connotation of these sites into new potential. Perhaps they can reveal another part of the city's identity.

Observing and analyzing the residual spaces raises awareness of the need for emptiness, a fundamental component in the process of making space. Recalling Rem Koolhaas' "strategy of the void," [1] the study of the city through the gaps, we are tempted to question an architecture that deals only with the solid and the tangible; that tries to fill in every space it encounters. How do those spaces in-between inform the way we build and use the city? This article intends to provide an overview of how contemporary architectural discourses use the term "void" as a theoretical concept, and how observation of two Hong Kong types of in-betweens has helped to broaden architectural knowledge and practice.

Genealogy

At an urban scale, voids that were not planned but appeared as scars resulting in urban transformation were starting to interest architects by the mid-Twentieth Century. Alison and Peter Smithson, from Team X, for example, categorized the voids as holes in the city, "made by the abandonment of sites and city centres, industrial dereliction, clearance by planners of historic centres, new connective systems that cut great swathes into the urban fabric." [2] A few decades later, in the book *Mutation,* [3] Rem Koolhaas highlighted the transformation of urban territories under the pressure of global economic restructuring. Socioeconomic changes have

struck everywhere: neo-liberal rationales have pervaded urban spaces and brought about a functional specification of all spaces, with the ascent of the two notions of "programme" and "event." [4] Both are, in fact, essential for Bernard Tschumi, who conceptualises the in-between as a residual – an interstice where unexpected events can happen. [5] Such a place doesn't result from a formal or aesthetic composition of space, but instead comes out of a programmatic logic. Instead of looking for coherence, for Tschumi, the role of the architect is to compose with the undefined and allow the mismatch to exist: "This extraordinary space derived from the concept [of in-between] appears as a "gift" or "supplement": a space where anything might happen; a place of experimentation; a place located on the margins." [6]

By the 2000s, a new generation of architects had expanded upon these visions and revealed a growing interest in understanding the city from what it rejects. In 2003, the Group E2 published *E2: exploring the urban condition* [7] and coined the term "in-between" after studying and working on the presence of "void spaces" in suburban areas of Paris. Their ideas were framed by a time of intensified globalisation, which led to the relocation of industries and the reorganisation of territories, guided by economic rationales. As a result, new unidentified shapes disseminated throughout territories imprinted on the urban fabric. [8] E2 explained that these spaces "generate ideas of instability, unadjustment, strangeness, imprecision, diversion, disorganisation, polymorphism, indeterminacy, complexity, trouble, incoherence. These ideas that create the conditions of uncertainty may lead to a feeling of discomfort, or to a form of curiosity." [9] For them, identifying such sites is before all else an opportunity to intervene, and the in-between a condition that triggers imagination.

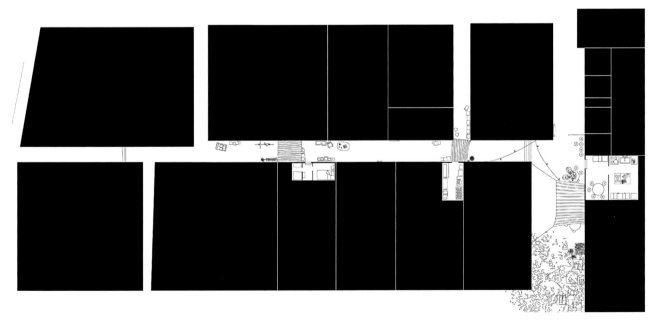

Back lane from above. Location: Tin Hau

Illegal activities in Tin Hau. Playing such games is forbidden in every Hong Kong's official public space.

A similar phenomenon of resultant voices can be observed in the contemporary Asian context. As Atelier BowWow explains in *Bow-Wow From Post-Bubble City*, the mutually reinforcing densification and fragmentation of the urban fabric in Tokyo has dramatically reduced the size of land plots.[10] Banal byproducts of this contemporary architectural practice in Japan, interstitial spaces are simply called 隙 間 – "sukima" (literally "gap space.")[11] Their morphological, legal, and temporal ambiguousness make them prime objects of interest for Yoshiharu Tsukamoto and Momoyo Kaijima of Atelier BowWow, who include 'gap spaces' within the development of their architecture. As they compose with these spaces, they manage to transform spatial constraints into an opportunity to make the inside spaces of their architecture interact with the contemporary urban context. "The fact that gap spaces will emerge in any case should be treated as feedback at the start of the design process, which I think is a strategy for designing small

buildings that only form a part of the metabolism of the existing city," states Tsukamoto.[12] Once identified, they are quickly adopted by architects who want to approach buildings in relation to their environment.[13]

In-betweens are also a programmatic expression of a transitional state. For example, in Japan, the idea of "in-betweenness" is embedded in architectural and cultural traditions. The programmatic thresholds, or transitional spaces, are accentuated by a search for materiality. This is notably illustrated by the omnipresence of the key concept of 間 – "ma," literally "a ray of moon passing through a gate" and commonly translated as "Japanese sense of place."[14]

The architectural components of the traditional Japanese house are developed and spatially arranged to reflect on a perception of space tightly connected to time and movement as expressed by the *ma*.[15] As a result, some spaces are conceived to bear the functions of both border and bond: the "engawa" (縁側

Transversal section through Hong Kong landmark in the background

—veranda), the "genkan" (玄関 - entrance) and the "shoji" (障子 - screen panels) will present the porous quality of elements that create transitions, as they are expected to "separate without completely cutting off the view."[16] In other words, the transformational condition of the space (or the capacity to create a total merging of inside and outside spaces) was primordial in the traditional Japanese house, and furniture elements were designed with the paramount purpose of permeability.[17]

However, the post WWII urban dynamic gradually erased this layering of porosity. Kazuhiro Kojima and Kazuko Akamatsu[18] point out that at this time, a new model of dwelling became massively adopted, namely the nLDK model (literally Living, Dining and Kitchen added to n number of bedrooms). While in traditional houses, rooms hosted a variety of activities, allowing for an overlap of functions, the nLDK's fixed program imposed a specific function on each space. In other words, over programming limited individual interpretation of place.

Interestingly, as transitional spaces disappeared in the realm of the private house, interstitial spaces seemed to concomitantly appear in between houses. These outdoor thresholds are therefore a useful material for the development of an architecture deeply embedded in the urban.

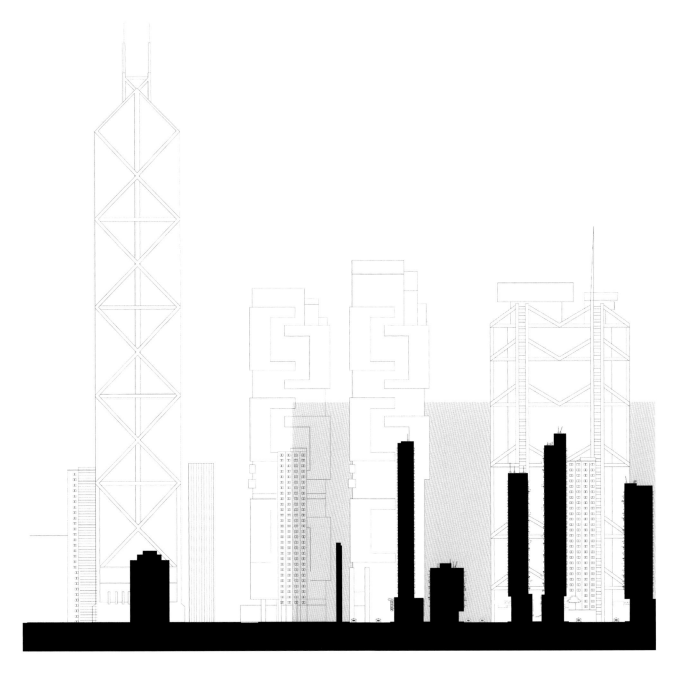

Transversal section through Wan Chai with Hong Kong landmark in the background

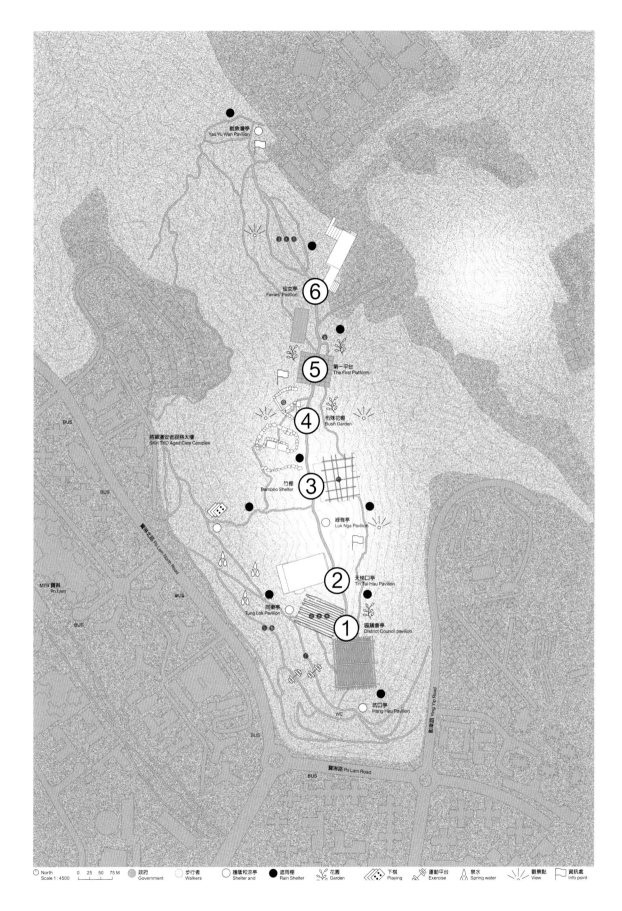

試魚灣亭
Yau Yu Wan Pavilion

仙女亭
Fairies' Pavilion

⑥

⑤ 第一平台
The First Platform

④ 布殊花棚
Bush Garden

將軍澳安老服務大樓
SKH TKO Aged Care Complex

③ 竹棚
Bamboo Shelter

綠雅亭
Luk Nga Pavilion

寶琳北路 Po Lam North Road

MTR 寶琳
Po Lam

② 天梯口亭
Tin Tai Hau Pavilion

同樂亭
Tung Lok Pavilion

① 圓議會亭
District Council pavilion

坑口亭
Hang Hau Pavilion

WC

寶琳路 Po Lam Road

英業路 Ying Yip Road

BUS

北
North
Scale 1 : 4500   0 25 50 75 M

政府
Government

步行者
Walkers

遮蔭和涼亭
Shelter and

遮雨棚
Rain Shelter

花園
Garden

下棋
Playing

運動平台
Exercise

泉水
Spring water

觀景點
View

資訊處
Info point

Hong Kong in–betweens

During the last decade, the focus of my research has been on understanding Asian cities' development mechanisms through the lenses of urban voids. Instead of looking at built forms, I studied the residual buffer zones and nonplanned spaces within the dense urban context of Hong Kong. These peculiar spaces forced curiosity and led to the development of analytical and design tools within my architecture office Parallel Lab. The tools, named the STAG project and the Duckling Hill newspaper, became agents to enquire into and navigate the in-betweens.

In-betweens in Hong Kong are narrow back lanes that form a network of interstitial spaces in the dense urban morphology. These narrow back streets are not registered on official maps however, put together, they represent an area of 150 square kilometers, four times the area of the recently reclaimed land that makes up the West Kowloon Cultural District. Although tiny in size, their recurrence in many urban areas has a strong impact on the way we perceive and experience the city. Less regulated and sterile than official public spaces (where one is welcomed by an arm long list of interdictions), these residual spaces – unplanned and appropriated by their inhabitants – function as important buffer zones across the city. When lack of space is an issue, these morphological in-betweens collect the overflow of life.

Inherent in the in–between condition is the ambiguity of ownership. In Hong Kong's back lanes, private activities overlap with public ground. A secondhand couch, potted plants, a mirror on a wall or T-shirts on hangers are indicators of a whole living system. Making the most out of the ambiguity of ownership, the network appears as a giant urban living room, configured to react to instant needs. Compared to official public spaces that are over regulated, the backlanes offer ground to all kinds of activities that would not usually be allowed in them: "and because the spaces are not saturated with function, there is room for appropriation."[19]

Within this territory of unwritten rules, space-appro-priators and passersby are shifting the lines of their personal boundaries. Because their forms are in constant negotiation between different users[20] the lack of clarity of ownership seems to call for consensus.

From these observations, it is possible to understand the connections between the different programs and to realise that in such a dense and harsh city, the types of interactions observed are similar to those you would expect to witness in a small village.

To further enquire into this ambiguous aspect of ownership, the observer had to become an actor. The STAG project, which included the design of a portable stool combined with a backpack, emerged as a type of experimentation with these ambiguities of time and ownership. The stool was the tool to reveal the unwritten rules. By organizing events (a tea ceremony, openair cinema, DJ party) in the interstices, temporary occupation led to negotiations with the neighbors and, occasionally, with the police, both scenarios prompting a recognition of the legitimacy of semiprivate uses on semipublic ground.

This unexpected outcome was an incentive to seek other ambiguous situations. The next case was that of a group of elderly people who, acting at another territorial scale, were engaged in a similar, subtle negotiation for domestication.

At the edge of Hong Kong's urban territory, the green slopes of Duckling Hill (鴨仔山) offer a natural buffer zone in which to escape from the standardised new town of Tseung Kwan O (將軍澳). Over the years, the local residents have gradually appropriated the hill and turned these slopes into their own public space. To facilitate access and enable a wide range of activities, they have built with great care a series of light interventions: stairs, resting spaces, flower gardens, self-made benches, pavilions and rubbish bins.

Once more, it is a matter of negotiation. Alleging safety concerns, the government of Hong Kong, uncomfortable with the idea of losing control, regularly makes claims on the land by eradicating the facilities. Yet, expecting this type of reaction from the authorities, the people of Duckling Hill have developed all sorts of strategies to circumvent the law. Among them: to mimic the appearance of official installations, and to dismantle and reassemble the pavilions, benches and staircases according to government warnings of destruction.

This situation shows another case of private use overlapping public ground. Behind the manicured flower garden, the set of hanging brooms, or the polished ground cleared of all leaves, we can sense a strong feeling of home, and the intimate relationship elders have with the hill. Their innate knowledge of the place's ecology puts them ahead of any team of experts. The question here is not "what to do" or "can we do it", but "how?" With direct testing on site, the design is never fixed and there is always room, in between the laws, for adaptation.

In their negotiation process with the authorities, the group of elders resorted to using a research team to convey their concerns. From researcher and designer, their role shifted to an agent inbetween the negotiating parties. Yet, rather than responding to their proposal to design a pavilion, the creation of a publication in the form of a newspaper, *The People of Duckling Hill*[21] aimed to voice every party's view on the Duckling Hill case.

Towards architecture

The term "inbetween" appears as a useful tool to refer to the residual and ambiguous buffer spaces found in the dense urban context. Interestingly, the level of uncertainty associated with this concept of in-between

illustrates a situation that seems difficult for architects to depict: in-betweens do not fall into the common categories of public/private, legal/illegal, indoor/outdoor, interior/exterior, and although they can be identified, they are often "given neither name nor shape"[22] and are not represented on official maps. Consequently, under one term, very different situations seem to cohabit. This ambiguity reflects how these spaces question the way we use and build the city.

From a user's perspective, over-programming and regulations upon public spaces mirror the authorities' need to control, and of non-definiteness. Thanks to their ambiguous status, these spaces provide multiple ways of interpretations and enable more intuitive forms of usage to emerge. Far from being a threat, this sense of domestication in a dense city encourages social coherence and stability: indeed, "who would want to destroy one's own living room?"[23]

Researchers are often expected to take a clear position. The question of whether to be for or against, to preserve or fix the spaces, is often asked. Once again, we cannot bear to live with ambiguity. In these cases, the researcher's role was to be an observer, acknowledging in-between spaces' existence as a city component that speaks about its status and needs. However, by revealing them the concomitant risk is to annihilate their in-between qualities. When the marginal begins to interest the authority – the planners and the developers – it immediately loses its allure as a refugee-zone, while the legitimate city simply soaks it up.

Six Duckling Hill walkers.
The core of regular Duckling Hill walkers, Tseung Kwan O residents aged between sixty and ninety years old, numbers around two hundred persons.

We must therefore understand this notion of in—between as a condition that thrives within the city, rather than one that adopts the superficial appearance of a leftover.

For an architect, observing these spaces is a rich source of inspiration that can lead to the reinvention of one's practice. In this overbuilt context, the role of the architect, designer, and planner is challenged; couldn't we be doing more than just filling gaps? Exploring this potential territory at different scales and scopes forces us to realise that neither guidelines nor designs would be able to reproduce the qualities held by such spaces. In essence, they cannot be planned.

Yet, if we should not intervene within them, and not try to create them, what should we do? Withdraw from any decision—making process and encourage a "laissez—faire" standpoint? Only by observing and understanding the city's mechanisms, can one truly evaluate where and where not to act, and allow this conversation to perpetuate.

ENDNOTES:

1 Rem Koolhaas, 'Strategy of the Void', in *S,M,L,XL* (New York: Monacelli Press, 1995), 602–62.

2 Alison Margaret Smithson and Peter Smithson, *The Charged Void: Urbanism* (New York: Monacelli Press, 2005).

3 Rem Koolhaas et al., *Mutations: Rem Koolhaas, Harvard Project on the City*. Stefano Boeri, Multiplicity, ed. Arc en rêve Centre d'Architecture (Barcelona: ACTAR, 2000).

4 Bernard Tschumi, *Bernard Tschumi: Architecture: Concept & Notation*, ed. Frédéric Migayrou and Aurélien Lemonier (Paris: Centre Georges Pompidou, 2014).

5 Bernard Tschumi and Joseph Abram, *Tschumi Le Fresnoy: Architecture In/Between* (New York: Monacelli Press, 1999).

6 Tschumi and Abram.

7 Groupe E2, ed., *E2: Exploring the Urban Condition* (Barcelona: ACTAR, 2003).

8 ibid

9 ibid

10 Atelier BowWow, *BowWow from PostBubble City* (Tokyo: INAX, 2006).

11 ibid

12 Tsukamoto, p.210 in Atelier BowWow.

13 Kitayama Koh, *Architectural Work. InBetween* (Tokyo: ADP, 2014).

14 Günter Nitschke, "'MA' The Japanese Sense of Place in Old and New Architecture and Planning," *Architectural Design*, March 1966, 113–56; and Arata Isozaki, *JapanNess in Architecture* (Cambridge, Mass: The MIT Press, 2006).

15 Mitsuo Inoue, *Space in Japan* (New York: Weatherhill, 1985).

16 Adrian Snodgrass, "Thinking Through the Gap: The Space of Japanese Architecture," *Architectural Theory Review 2*, no. 16 (2011): 136–56.

17 Nohirito Nakatani, ed., *Transition of Kikugetsutei, Equipment In Between,* Window Research Institute (Tokyo: YKK AP Inc., 2016).

18 Kazuhiro Kojima and Kazuko Akamatsu, *Essence Behind, Contemporary Architects' Concept Series 21* (Tokyo: LIXIL, 2016).

19 Géraldine Borio and Caroline Wüthrich, *Hong Kong InBetween*, Bilingual edition (Zürich: Park Books; Hong Kong: MCCM Creations, 2015).

20 ibid

21 Géraldine Borio and Caroline Wüthrich, *The People of Duckling Hill* (Hong Kong: Parallel Lab & Hong Kong Polytechnic University, 2014).

22 Atelier BowWow, *BowWow from PostBubble City*.

23 Borio and Wüthrich, *Hong Kong InBetween*

Exterior living room in a temporary illegal shelter located on the hill.

A spatial and urban narrative device known to be in use since antiquity, and revived in NY and Philadelphia in the '70s, is street art, and more specifically, graffiti art. This form of art stands between the illegal or informal (graffiti) and the commissioned and formal (community-based art projects such as murals), in which the nuances between art and vandalism unfold. Such divisions include comparisons that graffiti is word-based, whereas mural art is image-based. One is legal, and one illegal. One is relatable to society, and the other not. Both are forms of appropriation of the walls and surfaces of our existing environment, and carry the potential for social change. City surfaces appropriated with graffiti is art, experienced outside the galleries and museums for everyone. As Mieke Bal describes in her Introduction to *The Practice of Cultural Analysis: Exposing Interdisciplinary Interpretation*, graffiti is "exhibitionary in its creation and its display."[1] Similarly, Sonja Neef describes graffiti in her book *Imprint and Trace: Handwriting in the Age of Technology* as an ephemeral "live" performance rather than a permanent "inscription."[2]

Acts of sanctioned and unsanctioned inscriptions and exhibitions on the surfaces of our urban environment appear in the form of text and image in the existing space. Just like traditional exhibition design, urban surfaces act as a canvas for a new exhibit. However, in opposition to the museums and galleries, street art is about appropriating the existing, and in most cases, a rebellious and often dangerous (overnight) act. The narratives in street art can carry subversive statements meant for a single person, group or society at large as the piece "...is on show; and it shows itself, shows its hand, its presence."[3] The word "graffiti" itself describes stories of intervention as it derives from the Italian word *graffiato*, which means "scratched," and relates directly to works of art that are generated by scratching information into an existing surface. This act of scratching through a surface layer to reveal another layer beneath it reminds us of a palimpsest, a concept and metaphor used in Interior Architecture for leaving traces of information on surfaces such as walls and floors. The English roots of the word come from the Greek "graphein," meaning "to scratch, draw, and write."[4] With graffiti, the writing, rewriting, and transformation of our environment occurs.

In the book, *The City: Society and Politics in the Western City,* the author of the chapter "Graffiti as Territorial Markers" introduces a three dimensional aspect to graffiti art by examining the motives behind the 70's Philadelphia graffiti artist, Cornbread, and describes the entry of the artist into the site as "(t)he mastery and occupation of space."[5] Graffiti art is able to express a variety of social issues and establishes a relationship with the built heritage through visual communication. In between the past and the present, the temporary and the permanent, the surface and space, through the act of appropriation of the existing, graffiti creates a tension between the preservation of "what is" and the social and visual changes of what might still come.

ENDNOTES:

1 Mieke Bal, *The Practice of Cultural Analysis: Exposing Interdisciplinary Interpretation* (Stanford: Stanford University Press, 1999), 3-4.

2 Sonja Neef, *Imprint and Trace: Handwriting in the Age of Technology* (London: Reaktion Books, 2011), 281. 3 Ibid..

3 Mieke Bal, 4.

4 "Graffiti | Origin and Meaning of Graffiti by Online Etymology Dictionary". www.etymonline.com. Retrieved 2019-03-24

5 Michae Pacione, *The city: critical concepts in the social sciences* (London: Routledge, 2002) 169.

SCRATCH, DRAW AND WRITE

NARRATIVES ON URBAN CANVASES

by MARKUS BERGER

Title: *La que reparte el bacalao – The one that delivers the cod or the one with the final word* (2016)

Location: Monserrate St., Santurce, San Juan, Puerto Rico
6th Santurce es Ley, urban art festival

Artist: Dama Lola - Damaris Cruz

Photo: Markus Berger, 2016

The woman portrayed in the mural is selling street food, *bacalaítos fritos*, cod fritter, a very common scene in Puerto Rico. The phrase "the one with the final word" comes from the old custom in which the patriarch cut and distributed pieces of cod or meat among the family or employees. Playing with the native folklore to perpetuate culture, an essential part of Damaris Cruz's work is defined by the interaction with the people of the community. Her work creates interest in abandoned properties, highlighting the unnoticed architecture as part of the landscape and recovering the memory of the place.

Title: *Untitled*
Location: Donau Kanal, Vienna, Austria
Artist: Lush Sux,
Photo: Bwag

The Australian Graffiti Artist Lush Sux, known for his "meme-art" portraying known people and politicians created these two works at the Danube channel in Vienna.

Title: *INSIDE OUT*

Location: Times Square, New York City, USA, 2013

Artist: JR

Inside out New York City is part of the global art project titled *Inside Out*, by the French photographer JR. As in other places around the world, New Yorkers and visitors took self-portraits in a photo booth in Times Square. The printed portraits were pasted as posters on the streets in Times Square from April to May 2013. According to the artist's website, almost 6,000 people participated.

Title: *Face 2 Face*

Location: Israel & Palestine border wall

Artist: JR

Portraits of Israelis and Palestinians are pasted face to face on both sides of the wall to comprise the largest illegal photography exhibition ever. The project, aimed to draw out similarities between people on both sides, was carried out in several Palestinian and Israeli cities in 2007.

Title: *Unknown*
Location: Il Mattatoio, Piazza Orazio Giustiniani 4, Rome, Italy
Artist: Unknown,
Photo: Liliane Wong, 2008

The Mattatoio di Testaccio, before its conversion into spaces for the University of Rome, was an important architectural industrial heritage and former slaughter-house. At the time of the photo, it served as a shelter for the homeless.

Title: *GLASS HALF FULL*
Location: Cerra St., Bo. Santurce, San Juan, Puerto Rico, 2016
Artist: Fintan Magee (Australia)
Photo: Markus Berger

To raise awareness of the rising sea levels due to climate change and the impact it has over the Caribbean islands, a local boy is portrayed dressed for the beach carrying an iceberg on his bag pack. It is a reminder of what we are leaving as an inheritance for future generations and the global responsibility of the catastrophes suffered on the island.

Title: *And The Patterns Spoke of a Certain Certainty*
Location: Vienna, 2010
Artist: Addam Yekutieli
Photo: Boomshiva rasta

The city of Vienna declared the "Wiener Wand" (Vienna wall) as a legal surface for "Streetart." On one side of the Vienna Donau channel is Otto Wagner's Vienna Metropolitan Railway. The Vienna wall comprises graffiti and street art next to each, and on top of each other creating confusion between the legal, illegal art and vandalism. Addam Yekutieli, known for his work under the pseudonym Know Hope, creates work that lies between political situations and emotional conditions.

Title: *Chuuttt!!!* (2011)
Location: Place Igor Stravinsky, Beaubourg, Paris, France
Artist: Jef Aérosol (Jean-François Perroy)
Photo: Markus Berger, 2013

Described as a self portrait of the graffiti artist, the work titled *Chuuuttt !!!*, or Hush is a 300 square meter large wall mural right next to the Centre Pompidou

Title: *Hamburger* (c. 2013)
Location: Convalecencia Square, Juan Ponce de León Ave., Bo. Río Piedras, San Juan, Puerto Rico
Artist: Colectivo BASTA – BASTA Group, (Roberto Tirado, Javier Moreno and Jerone Zayas)
Photo: Markus Berger, 2016

The artists signed the mural as BASTA – Arte Contestatario (ENOUGH – Rebellious Art)
Former students of the Plastic Arts School in Old San Juan, the artists created resistance art against the colonial status. Adressing the suffering of the Puerto Rican working class controlled by the USA are dollars, cars, buildings, middle class workers in suits all residing within a fast food combo of hamburger, fries and soda.

Se Vende
(787)
423-4433

PROJECT CREDITS, INFORMATION AND BIBLIOGRAPHIES

EDITORIAL

Image Credits_ Markus Berger, 2016

INFORMAL ANNEXATIONS

Image credits_ All images courtesy by the author.

BIBLIOGRAPHY:

-Bruno, Marco, Simone Carena, and Minji Kim. *Borrowed City: Private Use of Public Space in Seoul*. Seoul: Damdi Publishing, 2015.

-Frampton, Adam, Jonathan D. Solomon, and Clara Wong. *Cities without Ground: A Hong Kong Guidebook*. Berkley: Oro Editions, 2015.

-Perrault, Dominique, Bernard Tschumi, Michel Desvigne, and Nasrine Seraji-Bozorgzad. *E2: Exploring the Urban Condition*. Paris: Groupe E2, 2002.

-Picon, Antoine. *Smart Cities: A Spatialised Intelligence*. Chichester: Wiley, 2015.

-Speck, Jeff. *Walkable City: How Downtown Can save America, One Step at a Time*. New York: North Point Press, 2013.

-Tarttara, Martino. "Brasilia's Prototypical Design" in *Architectural Design*, January/ February 2011, Volume 209.

HOLDING GROUND

Project Credits_ La Cité Arago, Saint Ouen, Architect: Paul Chemetov, 1975; La Maladrerie, Aubervilliers, Architect: Renée Gailhoustet, 1975-1986; La Cité des Francs-Moisins, Saint Denis, 1974; Quartier Pablo Picasso, Nanterre, Architect: Emile Aillaud, 1972-1981; Cité de L'Abreuvoir, Bobigny, Architect: Emile Aillaud, 1956-1958; All images courtesy by the author.

BIBLIOGRAPHY:

-Cupers, Kenny. *Housing Postwar France: The Social Project*. Minneapolis: University of Minnesota Press, 2014.

-De Sola Morales, Manuel. "La distance, Paramètre majeure de la composition complex" "Peripherie maudite ou Splendide", *Project Urbain*, N8 Mai 1996.

-Enright, Theresa.*The Making of Grand Paris: Metropolitan Urbanism in the Twenty-first Century*. Cambridge: MIT Press, 2016.

-Gaudard, Valerie, Florence Margo-Schwoebel and Benoît Pouvreau,1945-1975 *Une histoire de l'habitat : 40 ensembles de logements "Patrimoine du XXe siècle"*. Paris: Beaux Arts Editions, 2011.

-Klein, Richard, Gerard Hamel and Alex MacLean. *Les Grands Ensembles, Une Architecture du XXeme siecle*. Paris: Dominique Carré, 2011.

-*L'Esquive*. DVD, translated in English to *Games of Love and Chance*, Directed by Abdellatif Kechiche. 2002.

-Montale, Eugenio. *Selected Poems*. New York: New Directions Publishing Corporations, 1965.

-Ronai Simon. "Paris et la Banlieue: Je t'aime, moi non plus". *Herodote, Revue de Géographie et de Géopolitique*, second trimester, 2004.

PHANTOM MARKETS AND GHOST BOOTLEGGERS:

Image credits_ fig. 01. By Linden Claytor, Historical image by McClung Historical Collection; Fig. 02. By Author and McClung Historical Collection; Fig. 03. By Author; Fig. 04. By McClung Historical Collection; Fig. 05. by Linden Claytor, Historical Image of Market Square canopies by McClung Historical Collection.

RESTORATION IN HISTORICAL PERSPECTIVE

Image Credits_ Fig. 01. Temple-saturne-inscription.jpg (https://commons. wikimedia.org/wiki/File:Temple-saturne-inscription.jpg); Fig. 02. Alfonso Bartoli, I monumenti antichi di Roma nei disegni degli Uffizi di Firenze (Roma, 1914–22); fig. 03. Photo: University of Cologne, Arachne Project, BOOK-859121-0054_368478.jpg; fig. 04. AGE Fotostock America Inc.; fig. 05. The Conservatoire des Arts et Métiers, Paris: gateway and interior. Wood engraving by C.W. Sheeres after E. Shirond. Credit: Wellcome Collection. CC BY; fig. 06. Credit: Linda Hall Library of Science, Engineering & Technology

INVESTIGATIONS: BETWIXT AND BETWEEN

Image Credits_ Fig. 01-03. By Thomas Wilder; fig. 04. By Elaine Lopez and Adam Chuong; fig. 05. By Anna Albrecht; fig. 06. Chayandunks7 [CC BY-SA 4.0 (https://creativecommons.org/licenses/by-sa/4.0)], Chayandunks7 (https://commons.wikimedia.org/wiki/File:Jaali_eyes.jpg); Fig. 07-08. By Zhiqing Guo; fig. 09-10. By Gonzalo Nuñez Galetto.

ABSENT MATTER

Image Credits_ Fig. 01-10, © Roberto Conte; fig. 11-12, © Fabiano Caputo.

THE SONIFEROUS LANDSCAPE

Image Credits_ Fig. 01. Courtesy of Cunningham Dance foundation Archive; All other image courtesy by the authors;

BIBLIOGRAPHY:

-Cage, John. *Silence: Lectures and Writing*. Middletown: Wesleyan University Press, 1973.

-Corner, J. (2006). *Recovering landscape: Essays in contemporary landscape architecture*. New York: Princeton Architectural Press, 2006.

-Eisenman, Peter. "Visions Unfolding: Architecture in the Age of Electronic Media." *Domus* 734 (Jan 1992): 21-24.

-Gissen, David. "A More Monumental, Non-Naturalistic Environment." Newsom, Hannibal. In *Tarp Architecture Manual: Not Nature*, edited by Sarah Ruel-Bergeron, 51-53. Brooklyn: Pratt Institute, School of Architecture, 2012.

-Kant, Immanuel, and Werner S. Pluhar. *Critique of Judgment*. Indianapolis, Ind: Hackett, 2010.

-Krauss, Rosalind. "Photography's Discursive Spaces: Landscape/View." *Art Journal* 42, no. 4 (1982): 311-19. doi:10.2307/776691.

-Nesbitt, Kate. "The Sublime and Modern Architecture: Unmasking (An Aesthetic Of) Abstraction." *New Literary History* 26, no. 1 (1995): 95-110. http://www.jstor.org/stable/20057270.

-Nesbitt, Kate. *Theorizing a New Agenda for Architecture: An Anthology of Architectural Theory 1965-1995* (New York: Princeton Architectural Press, 2008).

-Pijanowski, Bryan C., Luis J. Villanueva-Rivera, Sarah L. Dumyahn, Almo Farina, Bernie L. Krause, Brian M. Napoletano, Stuart H. Gage, Nadia Pieretti, "Soundscape Ecology: The Science of Sound in the Landscape," *BioScience*, Volume 61, Issue 3 (1 March 2011): 203–216. https://doi.org/10.1525/bio.2011.61.3.6.

-Sakakeeny, Matt. *Keywords in Sound*. Durham: Duke University Press, 2015. ProQuest Ebook Central.

-Tate. "Sublime – Art Term." Tate. Accessed March 10, 2019. https://www.tate.org.uk/art/art-terms/s/sublime.

BETWEEN THE SACRED AND THE MUNDANE

Image Credits_ All images courtesy by the authors.

BIBLIOGRAPHY:

-Eck, Diana L. *Banaras: City of Light*. New York: Knopf, 1982.

-Khanna, Ashok and Ratnakar, Pramesh. *Banaras: The Sacred City*. New Delhi: Lustre Press, 1988.

-King, Richard. *Orientalism and Religion: Postcolonial Theory, India and 'The Mystic East'*, London: Taylor & Francis e-Library, 2001.

-Lannoy, Richard. *Benares Seen from Within*. London: John Martin, 1999.

-Shah, Tahir. "Varanasi, Benares, Banaras or Kashi, regardless its not an easy destination." *Indian Experiences: Discovering India Differently* (blog). May16, 2017. http://memsahibinindia.com/2017/05/11/snapshots-cremations-in-varanasi/

-Singh, Raghubir. *Banaras: Sacred City of India*. London: Thames and Hudson, 1987.

-Twain, Mark. *Following the Equator: A Journey around the World*. Hartford, 1897.

CULTURAL AMBASSADORS

Image Credits_ Fig. 01. https://commons.wikimedia.org/wiki/File:Huizhou_Xixinan_Laowuge_ji_Lüraoting_2016.11.13_16-55-13.jpg, https://creativecommons.org/licenses/by-sa/4.0/legalcode; fig. 02-03, 05-06, 10. Images courtesy by the author; fig. 04. https://www.flickr.com/photos/larry1732/38745928451/in/photostream/ Attribution 2.0 Generic (CC BY 2.0); fig. 07. Image permission by Mr. Jun Qiu; fig. 08. image permission by Wendao Garden Group; fig. 09. https://en.wikipedia.org/wiki/ Singapore_University_of_Technology_and_Design#/media/ File: Antique_Chinese_pavilion,_Singapore_University_of_Technology_and_Design_-_20150602-01.jpg

INTERSTITIAL PRACTICES

Image Credits_ fig. 01-02. Courtesy of Orizzontale;

BIBLIOGRAPHY:

-Bendiner-Viani, Gabrielle. "The Big World in the Small: Layered Dynamics of Meaning-making in the Everyday." *Environment and Planning D: Society and Space 31*, no. 4 (2013): 708-726.

-Brighenti, Andrea, ed. *Urban Interstices: The Aesthetics and the Politics of the In-between*. London: Routledge, 2013.

-Buber, Martin. "Das problem des Menschen (1943)." *Forum*, no. 8 (1959): 24.

-Carmona, Matthew. *Public Places-Urban Spaces: The Dimensions of Urban Design*. Oxford: Elsevier, 2003.

-Chevrier, Jean-François. *Des Territoires*. Paris: L'Arachnéen, 2011.

-Chidister, Mark. "Public Places, Private Life: Plazas and the Broader Public." *Places* 6, no. 1 (1989): 12-37.

-Doron, Gil. "The Dead Zone and the Architecture of Transgression." *City*, no. 4 (2000): 247-263.

-Eisenman, Peter. "Blue Line Text." In *Postmodernism: Critical Concepts* Vol. IV, edited by Viktor E. Taylor and Charles E. Winquist, 354-357. London: Routledge, 1998.

-Fredericks, Joel, Glenda Amayo Caldwell, and Martin Tomitsch. "Middle-out design: collaborative community engagement in urban HCI." In *Proceedings of the 28th Australian Conference on Computer-Human Interaction*, 200-204. Launceston: ACM, 2016.

-Gadanho, Pedro, ed. *Uneven Growth: Tactical Urbanisms for Expanding Megacities*. New York: MoMA, 2014.

-Hertzberger, Herman. *Lessons for Students in Architecture*. Rotterdam: 010 Publishers, 2005.

-Klanten, Robert, and Martin Hubner. *Urban Interventions: Personal Projects in Public Spaces*. Berlin: Gestalten, 2010.

-Lerner, Jaime. *Urban Acupuncture*. Washington: Island Press, 2016.

-Leveratto, Jacopo. "Planned To Be Reclaimed: Public Design Strategies for Spontaneous Practices of Spatial Appropriation." *Street Art & Urban Creativity Scientific Journal*, no. 1 (2015): 6-12.

-Lutzoni, Laura. "In-formalized Urban Space Design. Rethinking the Relationship between Formal and Informal," *City, Territory and Architecture* 3, no. 20 (2016), DOI 10.1186/s40410-016-0046-9.

-Lydon, Mike, and Anthony Garcia. T*actical Urbanism: Short-term Action for Long-term Change*. Washington: Island Press, 2015.

-Marcuse, Peter. "From Critical Urban Theory to the Right to the City." *City*, no. 13 (2009): 185-197.

-Mitchell, Don. *The Right to the City: Social Justice and the Fight for Public Space*. New York: Guilford, 2003.

-Piccinno, Giovanna, and Elisa Lega. *Spatial Design for In-between Urban Spaces*. Romagna: Maggioli, 2012.

-Piha, Helena. "Making Public Space. About the Same or About Difference?" *The Journal of Public Space 2*, no. 2 (2017): 145-180.

-Sadik-Khan, Janette. *Streetfight: Handbook for an Urban Revolution*. New York: Viking, 2016.

-Spirito, Gianpaola. *In-between places: Forme dello spazio relazionale dagli anni Sessanta a oggi*. Macerata: Quoldibet, 2015.

-Thomas, Alan. "Open Secrets." *Places Journal* (March 2010). https://doi.org/10.22269/100302.

-Van Eyck, Aldo. "Dutch Forum on Children's Home." *Forum*, no. 32 (1962): 602.

-Venturini, Gianpiero, and Carlo Venegoni, eds. *Re-Act: Tools for Urban Re-Activation*. Roma/Rezzato: Deleyva Editore, 2016.

-Wikström, Tomas. "Residual Space and Transgressive Spatial Practices – The Uses and Meanings of Un-Formed Space." *Nordisk arkitekturforskning 18*, no. 1 (2005): 47-68.

IN SEARCH OF SPATIAL NARRATIVES

Image credits _ Copyright of the paintings: © Fabien, reproduction by permission of Alain Gillis. The artwork was previously published in *Le Bazar du Génie* by Alain Gillis; Reproduction of illustrations courtesy of Alain Gillis (cf. note 27).

LOOKING FOR THE VOIDS IN-BETWEEN

Image credits_ fig. 01-05, by Parallel Lab; fig. 06-08, by Parallel Lab, Anaïs Boileau

SCRATCH, DRAW AND WRITE

Project credits_ fig. 01. Title: *La que reparte el bacalao – The one that delivers the cod or the one with the final word* (2016); Location: Monserrate St., Santurce, San Juan, Puerto Rico; 6th Santurce es Ley, urban art festival; Artist: Dama Lola - Damaris Cruz; Photo by Markus Berger, 2016; Project credits_ fig. 02. Title: *And The Patterns Spoke of a Certain Certainty*; Location: Vienna, 2010; Artist: Unknown; Photo by: Boomshiva rasta; (https://commons.wikimedia.org/wiki/File:Addam_Yekutieli_artwork_in_Vienna_2010.jpg), https://creativecommons.org/licenses/by-sa/4.0/legalcode; Project credits_ fig. 03. Title: *INSIDE OUT*; Location: Times Square, New York City, USA, 2013; Artist: JR; photo: JR (https://commons.wikimedia.org/wiki/File:InsideOutNYC-Times_Sq-138-JR.jpg), https://creativecommons.org/licenses/by-sa/4.0/legalcode; Project credits_ fig. 04. Title: *Face 2 Face*; Location: Israel & Palestine border wall; Artist: JR, copyright_ purchased by Gettyimages, number 73514419, photo by David Silverman; Project credits_ fig. 05. Title: *Unknown*; Location: Il Mattatoio, Piazza Orazio Giustiniani 4, Rome, Italy; Artist: Unknown; Photo by Liliane Wong, 2008; Project credits_ fig. 06. Title: *Glass half full* (2016); Artist: Fintan Magee (Australia); Location: Cerra St., Bo. Santurce, San Juan ; 6th edition of Santurce es Ley urban art festival; Photo by: Markus Berger, 2016; San Juan, Puerto Rico; Project credits_ fig. 07. Title: *Untitled*; Location: Donau Kanal, Vienna, Austria; Artist: Lush Sux, Photo by Bwag (https://commons.wikimedia.org/wiki/File:Wien_-_Donald-Trump-_und_Kim-Jong-un-Graffiti_von_Lush_Sux.JPG), https://creativecommons.org/licenses/by-sa/4.0/legalcode © Bwag/Wikimedia or © Bwag/Commons or © Bwag/CC-BY-SA-4.0; Project credits_ fig. 08. Title: *Chuuuttt !!!* (2011); Location: Place Igor Stravinsky, Beaubourg, Paris, France; Artist: Jef Aérosol (Jean-François Perroy); Photo by Markus Berger, 2013; Project credits_ fig. 09. Title: *Hamburger* (c. 2013); Location: Convalecencia Square, Juan Ponce de León Ave., Bo. Río Piedras, San Juan, Puerto Rico; Artist: Colectivo BASTA – BASTA Group, (Roberto Tirado, Javier Moreno and Jerone Zayas); Photo by Markus Berger, 2016

COLOPHON

Rana Abudayyeh is Assistant Professor of Interior Architecture at the University of Tennessee, Knoxville. She is a licensed architect in her native country, Jordan, where she is currently researching patterns of forced displacement while examining current forms of interior spatiality in refugee camps. Abudayyeh's pedagogical interests focus on advancing new modes of architectural production employing computational design, digital fabrication, and novel material logics. She seeks to define innovative design trajectories rooted in a site-based approach that responds to various contextual layers.

Puja Anand is an Interior Designer as well as Associate Professor and course leader within the Post Graduate Interior Design and Styling Department in the School of Design at Pearl Academy, New Delhi. Her work focuses on the traditional culture of India and the application of cultural crafts in interiors and spaces, with the belief that the contemporary application of crafts in modern interiors can help sustain the rich heritage and culture of India.

Alok Bhasin is an Architect and Interior Designer with over twenty-two years of professional experience in India and abroad. Alok is an Associate Professor within the Post Graduate Interior Design and Styling Department in the School of Design at Pearl Academy, New Delhi. His research centers around arts, culture, history of design, traditional craft heritage and sustainability.

Géraldine Borio is a Swiss Registered Architect, MArch EPFL, Assistant Professor at The University of Hong Kong, Department of Architecture, and Ph.D. candidate at the Royal Melbourne Institute of Technology. The gaps, voids and so-called 'resultant spaces' of Asian cities have been her entry points to understand the mechanisms of the built environment. Co-funder of Parallel Lab, Géraldine's research and architecture-based practice has evolved across multiple scales, shifting from in-situ observation and intervention to the making of space. She is the coauthor of the books *Hong Kong In¬Between* (2015) and *The People of Duckling Hill* (2014).

Madalina Ghibusi is an Architect and Teaching Assistant in the School of Architecture, Urban Planning and Construction Engineering at Politecnico di Milano. In 2016, she began a Ph.D. in the Architectural, Urban and Interior Design Program of the Politecnico, where she conducts research regarding the socio-psychological implications of urban public spaces. In 2018, she co-edited the book *Urban Design Ecologies: Projects for City Environments*, which focuses on coagulating urban strategies from multi-disciplinary perspectives upon urban environments.

Philip Jacks is Professor of Art & Architectural History at George Washington University and previously taught at Yale University. He earned his Ph.D. at the University of Chicago and Masters of Architecture at University of Maryland. Dr. Jacks has received fellowships from the Fulbright, Kress Foundation (Bibliotheca Hertziana), and Dumbarton Oaks. His books include *The Antiquarian and the Myth of Antiquity: The Origins of Rome in Renaissance Thought* and *The Spinelli of Florence: Fortunes of a Renaissance Merchant Family*. He served as editor for Giorgio Vasari, *Lives of the Most Excellent Painters, Sculptors and Architects* and *Vasari's Florence: Artists & Literati at the Medicean Court*. His forthcoming book, '*To Make it a Grand Entrepot': the Story of Locust Point, Baltimore*, explores the urban impact of grain elevators across the 19th century.

Jacopo Leveratto, PhD is Adjunct Professor of Interior Architecture in the School of Architecture, Urban Planning and Construction Engineering at Politecnico di Milano and a Research Fellow at the Department of Architecture and Urban Studies of the same university. His research focuses on public space design, with emphasis on urban habitability and the human dimension of planning. He is also a Correspondent for *Op.Cit.* and the Associate Editor of the peer-reviewed international book series *ii inclusive interiors* and the peer-reviewed journal *iijournal_International Journal of Interior Architecture and Spatial Design*.

Rafael Luna is Assistant Professor at Hanyang University and co-founder of the architecture firm PRAUD. He received a Master of Architecture from Massachusetts Institute of Technology. Luna's current research focuses on infra-architectural hybrid typologies as systems for urban efficiency. Luna is the award winner of the Architectural League Prize 2013, and his work has been exhibited at the MoMA in New York, Venice Biennale, Seoul Biennale, as well as published internationally. He has professional experiences in Japan (Toyo Ito), UK (KPF), France (Ateliers Jean Nouvel), and the US (Martha Schwartz Partners, dECOi, Sasaki Associates, and Machado and Silvetti). He is currently pursuing his Ph.D. research on Infra-architectural typologies at L' Accademia di architettura in Mendrisio, Switzerland. He is the co-author of, *I Want to Be Metropolitan*, and editor of the *North Korean Atlas*.

Andreas Müller is a self-employed editor, translator, and writer based in Berlin, Germany. He contributes to the conceptual planning, project management, and editing of publications in architecture and related fields. As a translator, he contributed to the German editions of Ada Louise Huxtable's *The Tall Building Artistically Reconsidered* and Anthony Vidler's *Claude-Nicolas Ledoux*. As a writer, his work centers around images as spaces of representation. Among his publications are *Berlin Schauplätze* (Berlin: Ullstein, 1986) and "Forethoughts to a strategy of print and digital publishing" (in German, www.boersenblatt.net/bookbytes, 2018). He studied History and German Languages at Freie Universität Berlin, the Sorbonne, and Washington University in St. Louis, Missouri.

Pari Riahi is a Registered Architect and Assistant Professor at the University of Massachusetts Amherst in the Department of Architecture. She completed her PhD at McGill University in 2010 and taught at the Rhode Island School of Design, Massachusetts Institute of Technology, and SUNY Buffalo before coming to UMass. Her research is centered on architectural drawings, representation and contemporary cities in crisis; her work sits at the confluence of landscape, urban, and architectural design. Her first book, *Ars et Ingenium: The Embodiment of Imagination in Francesco di Giorgio Martini's*

Drawings (Routledge, 2015) concerns the systematic inclusion of drawing as a component of architectural design, while her upcoming book, *Disjointed Continuity: Architectural Drawing in the Post-Digital Era* tracks the propagation of digital media and its effect on architectural theory and practice. Prior to starting her practice in 2011, Pari worked for the offices of Machado and Silvetti and Martha Schwartz Inc. Her office focuses on small-scale built projects as well as large-scale hypothetical interventions within the confines of cities.

Liz Teston is a designer and Assistant Professor of Interior Architecture at the University of Tennessee, Knoxville. Teston's teaching and research is situated at the intersection of urban interiority, design politics, and cultural identity. She is the current CoAD Dudley Faculty Scholar (2017-19) and was a Fulbright Scholar in Bucharest, Romania (2018). She has published works in the *Interior Architecture Theory Reader, MONU, International Journal of Interior Architecture + Spatial Design*, with forth coming contributions to *Interior Futures* (anticipated 2019), *Transient Spaces* (anticipated 2020) and *Interior Urbanism Reader* (anticipated 2020).

Hongjiang Wang, is an interior Architect, Associate Professor at the Department of Environmental Design of Shanghai Institute of Visual Arts and a doctoral candidate of Shanghai University. He focuses his research on two topics: "Narrative Space Design of Children's Healing Environment" on the conversion of medical space to healing space in China; "Design for urban sightseeing ship" on mobile landscape construction in urban rivers via narrative. He is in charge of the fund-supported research "Interactive Public Arts in Children's Healing Environment" aimed to develop new narrative spatial device, process and system strategies to strength services for children.

Anne West is a writer, theorist, and independent curator as well as Senior Lecturer in the Division of Graduate Studies at Rhode Island School of Design. Known for fostering rich cross-disciplinary learning environments of inquiry, team building and influence, she teaches a range of seminars including *Investigations: Betwixt and Between*. West is author of *Mapping the Intelligence of Artistic Work* and recipient of RISD's John R. Frazier Award for Excellence in Teaching. She holds a Ph.D.in Arts and Media Studies from the University of Toronto, Canada, with a research practice in phenomenology, poetics, and interpretive human studies.

Kramer Woodard (posthumous author) was a practicing architect in Albuquerque, NM and Professor at the University of New Mexico, School of Architecture & Planning. He was also the creator and principal designer of S³, a prefabricated building system for which he holds patents. His work has been widely published and acknowledged through numerous awards, books and magazines. He has lectured throughout the U.S. and other parts of the world, and held teaching positions at the Royal Melbourne Institute of Technology, Columbia University, Rice University, University of Texas, Austin, and Pratt Institute.

EDITORS

Ernesto Aparicio is a Senior Critic in the Department of Graphic Design at RISD. Aparicio earned his BA at the Escuela de Bellas Artes, La Plata, Buenos Aires and completed his Post Graduate Studies at the Ecole des Art Decoratifs, Paris. Prior to moving to the US, he served as Art Director for Editions du Seuil in Paris, while maintaining his own graphic design practice, Aparicio Design Inc. Best known for his work in the world of publishing, Aparicio has worked on corporate identities, publications, and way-finding for corporations and institutions in France, Japan, and the US. Recently, Aparicio was named Creative Director for the New York firm DFA.

Markus Berger is Associate Professor and Graduate Program Director in the Department of Interior Architecture at RISD. Berger holds a Diplomingenieur für Architektur from the Technische Universität Wien, Austria and is a registered architect (SBA) in the Netherlands. Prior to coming to the US, Berger practiced and taught in the Netherlands, Austria, India, and Pakistan. He currently heads *THE REPAIR ATELIER*, an art and design studio that engages in the innovative reuse and remaking of everyday objects, existing spaces and buildings through forms of repair. His work, research, writing, and teaching focus on art and design interventions in the built environment, including issues of sensory experience, forms of interventions and repair. He is a co-founder and co-editor of the *Int|AR Journal*.

Liliane Wong is Professor and Head of the Department of Interior Architecture at RISD. Wong received her Masters of Architecture from Harvard University, Graduate School of Design and a Bachelor of Art in Mathematics from Vassar College. She is a registered Architect in Massachusetts and has practiced in the Boston area, including in her firm, MWA. She is the author of *Adaptive Reuse_Extending the Lives of Buildings*, co-author of *Libraries: A Design Manual* and contributing author of *Designing Interior Architecture and Flexible Composite Materials in Architecture, Construction and Interiors*. A long time volunteer at soup kitchens, she emphasizes the importance of public engagement in architecture and design in her teaching. Wong is a co-founder and co-editor of the *Int|AR Journal*.

MDES Interior Studies [Adaptive Reuse]

The 2+ year Master of Design (MDes) in Interior Studies [Adaptive Reuse] provides a unique design education on the alteration of existing structures through interior interventions and adaptive reuse. The program establishes a clear aesthetic, theoretical and technological framework for the study of interior studies and adaptive reuse. Graduating students are properly equipped to engage in this subject in the general design field and to develop strategies in their work which recognize the importance of social and environmental responsibility.

MDES Interior Studies [Exhibition & Narrative Environments]

The study of Exhibition and Narrative Environments has been a part of the studio offerings of the Department of Interior Architecture for many years. The department has hosted annual studios specific to the design of the narrative environment that featured collaborations with the key members of the RISD Museum, the RISD Departments of Graphic Design, History of Art & Visual Culture and Brown University, in particular, the Haffenreffer Museum and the John Nicholas Brown Center. The Exhibition and Narrative Environments track consists of an MDes curriculum supported by courses offered in these other disciplines, formalizing the existing relationships with these departments.

MA Adaptive Reuse

Formerly called "MA Interior Architecture [ADAPTIVE REUSE]", the purpose of the Master of Arts (MA) in Adaptive Reuse is to provide a unique specialist design education on the subject of adaptive reuse as a post-professional study to a first degree in Architecture. The program aims to establish a clear aesthetic, theoretical and technological framework for the study of adaptive reuse, in order that graduating students are properly equipped to engage in the practice of working with existing buildings, structures and spaces. It enables students to develop strategies in their work which recognize the importance of social and environmental responsibility.

BFA Interior Studies [Adaptive Reuse]

The BFA is centered on rethinking the life of existing spaces – through design alterations, renovations and adaptive reuse, but encompasses also a very wide range of studies that engage with existing fabric, from installation design and retail design to more traditional interior design.

Int|AR

A decade of Int|AR

Vol. **01** "Inaugural Issue"
2009, (out of print)
co-editors: Markus Berger, Heinrich Hermann and Liliane Wong

Vol. **02** "Adapting Industrial Structures"
2011, ISBN: 978-0-9832723-0-4
co-editors: Markus Berger, Heinrich Hermann and Liliane Wong

Vol. **03** "Emerging Economies"
2012, ISBN: 978-0-9832723-1-1
co-editors: Markus Berger, Liliane Wong
Associate Editor Maya Marx

Vol. **04** "Difficult Memories: Reconciling Meaning"
2013, ISBN: 978-0-9832723-2-8
co-editors: Markus Berger, Liliane Wong

Vol. **05** "Resilience and Adaptability"
2014, ISBN 978-3-03821-606-3
co-editors: Markus Berger, Liliane Wong
Special Editor: Damian White

Vol. **06** "The Experience Economy"
2015 ISBN:978-3-03821-984-2
co-editors: Markus Berger, Liliane Wong
Special Editor: Jeffrey Katz

Vol. **07** "Art in Context"
2016 ISBN:978-3-0356-0834-2
co-editors: Markus Berger, Liliane Wong
Special Editor: Patricia Philips

Vol. **08** "Water as Catalyst"
2017 ISBN:978-3-0356-1197-7
co-editors: Markus Berger, Liliane Wong

Vol. **09** "Intervention as Act"
2018 ISBN:978-3-0356-1608-8
co-editors: Markus Berger, Liliane Wong
Special Editor: Nick Heywood